1,001
Ways to Market Yourself
and Your Small Business

1,001
Ways to Market Yourself and Your Small Business

Lisa Shaw

A Perigee Book

A Perigee Book
Published by The Berkley Publishing Group
200 Madison Avenue
New York, NY 10016

Copyright © 1997 by Lisa Shaw
Book design by Rhea Braunstein
Cover design by Joe Lanni

First edition: August 1997

Published simultaneously in Canada.

The Putnam Berkley World Wide Web site address is
http://www.berkley.com

Library of Congress Cataloging-in-Publication Data
Shaw, Lisa Angowski Rogak.
    1,001 ways to market yourself and your small business / Lisa
Shaw.
        p.   cm.—(a Perigee book)
    ISBN 0-399-52314-6
    1. Marketing.   2. Small business—Management.   I. Title.
HF5415.S414   1997
658.8—dc21   96-46295
                                                      CIP

Printed in the United States of America

10 9 8 7 6 5 4 3 2

For my cats
Mister Pippy,
Rula Lenska,
Miss Bunny,
Mister Mush,
Squatter, and
Miss Sugar Bombe,
and the late, great Margo and Squggy,
who have taught me that the only way to market is to
forge full speed ahead,
and to not give a whit what it looks like . . .

CONTENTS

～

INTRODUCTION

All too often, the idea of marketing makes even the most fearless fledgling entrepreneur uncomfortable. Nevertheless, it's one aspect of running a business that you need to understand and to use wisely in order to survive.

What does marketing mean to you? Most people think advertising, and not much else. If all you can envision is expensive, glossy ad campaigns on TV and in national magazines, or you think that the boys (and girls) on Madison Avenue have cornered the market on ways to get customers, you can take heart from the ideas and anecdotes you'll find in these pages. Not only will you find the nuts and bolts of publicity, advertising, networking, and the other components that make up marketing, you'll also discover hundreds of innovative ways that small business owners just like you have made their businesses prosper.

You don't need a degree in marketing to sell your business effectively. In fact, you're probably able to sell it better than a professional because you know your business best. Sometimes professional marketers get stuck in a herd mentality. Perhaps they've all been reading the same textbooks on marketing strategies for the big, rich, and powerful corporations that have little relevance for the average small-business owner. And, curiously, innovative thinking is often absent from the big agencies and corporations that have the most money to spend. The source for many of the ideas in this book is small- and medium-size businesses across the country that have had to cope with limited money and time.

Most important, you bring to the selling of your business the passion that can't be bought with even the biggest ad budget. Just as no one else will handle your customers the way you will, you're the best person to promote your business because no one is going to care about your business as much as you do.

I hope that this book will give direction to your own creative drive and provide a framework upon which to build the kind of advertising, publicity, and marketing that's right for your business.

The best way to use this book is to browse through the pages to read about the myriad ideas that have worked for others. Many of these ideas may have already occurred to you. You may even have tried some with varying degrees of success. Others may be completely new for you— and sometimes might appear to be a little crazy—but they frequently do work.

If you've already slogged through the tedious aspects of getting a business up and running, then I guarantee that this will be the fun part. The only limitations you have are the ones you set yourself. And if even just one of the ideas in this book works for you then the modest investment you've made today will pay you back many times!

So have fun and get out there and market your business.

DEVELOPING YOUR MARKETING PLAN

1. Like having a business plan, it's important that you develop some kind of marketing plan so you'll have a blueprint to follow in the months ahead, as well as a way to evaluate what has worked for you in the past, in addition to what hasn't.

2. When drawing up your marketing plan, make sure that you have enough lead time for the special events and promotions that you're planning. For instance, it's never too early to think about Christmas where national magazines are concerned. In fact, the best time to send a press kit to a national magazine about your annual activities is in July. Just be sure to send photos from last year's holiday celebrations.

3. Developing a marketing plan can be a simple task consisting of writing up the goals you'd like to achieve in the next six to twelve months or a complicated one, containing market and revenue projections as well as the percentage of the market you'd like to assume from your competitors.

Getting Started

4. Make a list of the first twenty-five things that come into your mind when you think about the purpose of your business. Don't edit as you go; instead, write down everything that you think of. Then, take the most outrageous item and design a plan to market your business around it. This exercise will inevitably stimulate creative thinking and breed lots of new ideas.

5. The name of your business, product, or service should include a benefit to the customer.

6. In twenty-five words or less, describe your business and the benefits that it offers to your customers. Then gear all your marketing toward this. Make up several signs with the twenty-five words, then tack them up where both you and your employees can see them on a regular basis.

7. Before you decide upon marketing strategies you need to determine your customer profile. Draw up a profile of what you envision to be your typical customer: Where does he live? What does he do for a living? How much does he make? What does he drive? What does he do in his spare time, etc. This will help you determine the best way to reach your customer and to develop your marketing plan.

8. Using the categories in this book, make a list of the tools you will use to market your business to new and existing customers.

Refining Your Marketing Plan

9. Define your image. If you don't know what it is, how do you expect to be able to tell your customers and potential customers? Ask yourself the following questions: What is special about my business? What do I offer that my competitors don't? Who are my customers? What's the main reason customers give for coming back to me? Why don't they come back?

10. How are you different from your competitors? It's possible to build an entire marketing plan based just on one small difference. Whether it's price, convenience, or your late hours, take advantage of it and go from there.

11. To some consumers, speed is the most important benefit that a business can offer. Think about how you can serve this rapidly growing group of customers.

12. Develop a focus group of your colleagues and potential customers to review your aims and predictions to gain valuable feedback.

13. Any component of your marketing plan can be changed at any time. You will always want to be refining the way you do business and how you present yourself—whether it's a new logo or refocusing your whole business in response to a changing economic climate. But always keep the customer in mind so you don't lose her along the way.

14. You can be inspired by the marketing ideas that others have used successfully, but these should always be tailored to your specific needs.

15. If you've been in business for a while, perhaps the most drastic way to turn your business around is to change its name. Keep everything else the same, but make your new name reflect service and attention to your customers.

16. If you're just starting out in business, focus on one specific market and then promote only to this group. For instance, if you think that working mothers would benefit most from your gourmet take-out shop, then target them in the places they're most likely to be and the media they're mostly likely to pay attention to.

17. Hire others to do your "grunt" work as soon as your business can afford it: for example, order fulfillment can be handled by a fulfillment house, freeing you to develop other aspects of your business.

18. Survey your staff for marketing ideas. If they're appropriate for your business, let the employees who came up with the ideas carry them out under your supervision. Pay for all expenses, and hold a monthly contest for the best idea. They may surprise you.

Your Marketing Budget

19. If you sell a product through a variety of retailers, wholesalers, and distributors, allocate a portion of the marketing budget that you include in your marketing plan to promote your products not only to consumers but also to these businesses that sell your product to customers.

20. One common adage in the field of marketing goes like this: One line in the editorial section is worth at least ten lines of advertising. Consider this formula when drawing up your marketing plans in terms of time and budget.

21. Through the grapevine or through estimates of the amount of advertising you see, try to figure out how much your competitors spend on marketing. Make sure you allot at least as much as they're spending.

22. How much do you spend to acquire each new customer? How much do you spend to keep him or her? Use this to figure out your marketing budget for the following year.

23. When planning your marketing budget for the upcoming year, figure on spending anything from 5 to 10 percent of gross sales. If you're in a business with a high profit margin, your marketing costs will veer toward the top end of that scale.

24. Whenever you bring out a new product or service, always be sure to chart the revenues it generates on a month-to-month basis. Every product and service has a natural time line where sales build slowly, achieve some momentum, and then peak before falling. If your sales begin to fall, it may not mean that you've reached market saturation; instead, it could mean that you need to make an extra push in your marketing. So before you discontinue a product or service to start another, make sure that you've done all you can to promote the existing product or service.

25. If your budget limits you to choosing either $1,000 worth of advertising or $1,000 worth of direct mail, choose the latter. Direct mail will not only generate more orders but also help you determine exactly where those orders are coming from. Advertising may boost the amount of traffic in your store or increase the number of phone inquiries. Advertising also tends to build name recognition more than direct sales.

Scheduling

26. If you've been in business for more than a year, you should be familiar with the cycles of business activity. Your strategies for year two should take advantage of downtime for routine tasks, catch-up, etc.

27. Thanks to book marketing expert John Kremer for this next gem: Every day, try to make just five new contacts to promote your business. Whether it's calling an editor, sending out a press release to a new publication, or faxing a copy of an article to a radio producer, these are things that don't take long to do but the positive effect can really add up quickly when you do just five of them a day.

28. Budget plenty of time for market research—the more you know about your business, the competition, your customers (and potential customers), the economic environment, the more effective your decision on where to spend your marketing dollars will be.

29. If you're having trouble finding the time to market your business, either set aside a five-hour period once a week—and hire someone else to answer the phone for the afternoon—or set a goal to accomplish one marketing task each day. For instance, send out letters to five people who have just become new customers to thank them, or send notes and information to five different editors, writers, or producers.

30. No matter how busy you are, set aside a block of time to devote to marketing. Pick the way to spend your marketing time that works best for you—whether it's an hour a day, or one solid afternoon a week—and then treat that time as sacred with no interruptions.

31. Whenever you plan a big promotion, make sure that, a month before, you check to see that you have enough items in stock or staff on hand to handle the response. Running out of an item or not having enough people to help during a big promotion could do more to dampen your future marketing programs than just about anything else.

Testing Your Idea

32. Before you roll out a new product to the public, do some informal test marketing by bringing samples to the owners of some local businesses to get some honest feedback. People love to think of themselves as experts, and it's likely that you'll be able to get a lot of valuable advice from the very people who are in the position to help you to sell your product.

33. Once you have completed the writing of your latest marketing plan, give it to everyone in your company. You might also want to include freelancers. Not only will this help your staff to get a better idea of your focus, it should also help solicit a number of new ideas that only they can give based on their perspective of working in your business.

34. When deciding which of your many marketing ideas to launch first, pick the one or two that seem the most fun. This will inevitably breed success, which will make you feel more confident about tackling the other items on your list.

35. Give these ideas your own unique twist. For example, pick up your favorite magazine and leaf through it with an eye toward how your business would fit into each section. For example, in the magazine *Country Living*, the section "Cross Country" is a travel grab bag of sorts while "Save Our Countryside" is a digest of environmental news. Many rural businesses could fit into either section with ease, so it's worth taking the time to project your business into a variety of sections in one magazine.

Give It Time!

36. Give your current marketing plan at least six months to show results. So dig in your heels and don't fix it until you know for sure it's broken.

37. Try to review your marketing plan at least once every month. Check your progress against your marketing efforts of the last month. At the same time, work the tasks you've planned for the next month into your day-to-day schedule.

38. For the next three months, focus all your marketing on one specific group, whether it's your house list or a new target group. Track your results for the following six months to see how this precision increases your business.

39. After you successfully accomplish one of the marketing aspects of your plan, be sure to reward yourself in some way, whether that means a dinner out or choosing an idea that is even more fun than the one you just finished.

MARKETING MATERIALS

You frequently hear people say that it's the first impression that counts the most. When it comes to the materials that you use to market yourself and your small business—from brochures to business cards—this is certainly true.

People today are inundated with an overabundance of marketing materials that come at them from all directions. After a very short while, most just learn to tune it out. That's why it's important to take extra care in planning and assembling the items you use to promote your business: if you attract people with your marketing materials, you're on the way to developing long-term, appreciative customers.

Content

40. If you produce a newsletter to promote your business to existing customers, be sure to include an article or some statistics in it that will help peg you as an expert and therefore produce some media interest. For instance, a personal organizer and shopper in Massachusetts produces a two-page newsletter that contains information on fashion and statistics. As a matter of course, she sends copies of the newsletter with her press kit to the media; a few reporters picked up on the statistics, quoting her company as the source. For Mary Lou Andre, the founder of Organization by Design, it all snowballed from there, culminating in a regular spot on the Home Shopping Network.

41. If you want to write compelling headlines for your marketing materials, check out the *Wall Street Journal*. Often, the editors will offer up a bit of wit that is slightly tongue in cheek but that makes you want to read the story. "Baskets in Small Town Ohio" is boring. But try this: "Dresden, Ohio, Puts All Its Eggs in Baskets, Especially a Big One." Of course, your curiosity is piqued.

42. If your business is unusual either in itself or for your area, your promotional materials should stress your uniqueness. Your copy should also appeal to a potential customer's unique needs and taste as well.

43. Testimonials in your marketing materials need to demonstrate exactly *how* your product or service helped the customer. General laudatory comments are not as effective for selling as citing specific benefits.

44. If you do business on both a local and national basis, make sure that you print your local phone number in all your marketing materials aimed toward your neighborhood. For national markets, of course, you should include just your 800 number.

45. Deliberately make some mistakes, either in your promotional materials or around your place of business, and challenge customers and prospective customers to find them. Reward the winners with discount coupons and/or free samples.

46. If you've designed a poster to promote your business that includes tear-off tags with your phone number at the bottom, be sure to include the name of your business as well as a line that describes you in more detail on each tag. Otherwise, people will see your number but probably not remember what it's for.

47. If you've developed an advisory board for your business, you may want to put a list of the board's members on your stationery. This is especially important if you send letters to potential customers who may not be familiar with your business.

48. If your business is family-friendly, don't miss simple marketing opportunities: Develop brochures or other promotional materials that are aimed directly at children. Use bright colors and bold graphics and make the copy easy to read. Include a section in the brochure for parents about the special things that your business does for kids.

49. If you're in one of the building trades or otherwise must be licensed in order to do business in your state, be sure to include your license number in all your promotional materials. This will immediately add to your credibility in the eyes of prospective customers.

50. Many potential customers will see your small size as an asset. Play up this theme of "small is better" in all your marketing materials; doing so will immediately imply a small-business owner's pride in personalized service and superior products and services.

51. In your promotional copy, remember that each adjective you use will conjure up a subjective image in the minds of prospective customers. For instance, the term *luxury* means different things to different people. Better to focus on nouns, facts, and numbers.

52. If you belong to one or more associations, from the Chamber of Commerce to the professional association for your field, publicize that fact on all your marketing materials. Your business will be legitimized not only for members of these associations but also for general consumers for whom these groups represent professionalism.

53. One of the most effective ways to describe the benefits of your product or service is to feature them as a bulleted or checkmarked list. Of course, you should make sure that each benefit is described as clearly as possible.

54. To ensure that prospects read through your marketing piece in its entirety, end each page with a sentence that runs onto the next page. It is possible to make these turnover sentences intriguing enough to convince the reader to continue, like . . . "In only ten days you can double your money."

55. Promote your business by stressing the ways that you can help your customers save time, or at least make it seem as if they have more of it. Since the lack of time seems to be a number-one frustration in most consumers' lives, saving them time can be more important than saving them money.

56. If your business primarily targets one specific audience, it may also help to mention the kinds of people to whom your business will *not* appeal. This may lend your product or service an appealing air of exclusivity among your customers.

57. Unless you've just opened for business, any information you provide about your company should include the *year* it started.

58. If you offer gift certificates, be sure to promote them in all your literature.

59. What is the number-one thing that your customers tell you they enjoy about your business? Use that as your headline in all ads and promotional material, get testimonials if appropriate, and then use them judiciously. In another year, ask them again and repeat.

60. Give your promotional copy a sense of urgency. Whether it's a limited-time offer or seasonal promotion, always make sure you give your audience a reason to respond *now*.

Selecting the Style and Tone of Your Marketing Materials

61. Always direct your advertising and marketing materials as if you're speaking to one person at a time. Make each reader feel special. Write everything in the second person, and in some cases it won't hurt to use a somewhat conspiratorial tone.

62. Proofread every piece of written material that you send out. No matter how beautiful a sales piece may be, people will judge your business by your attention to detail, or the lack of it.

63. Before you sign off on any promotional piece directed toward customers or the media, go over it once more to make sure that all the text presents the facts about your business in a positive light. This also means assuming a positive frame of mind concerning your competitors, a note of grace that will earn you respect in these cutthroat days.

64. Don't be afraid to be controversial when preparing any of your marketing materials. Taking a position that is the opposite of the popular viewpoint will help attract the attention of the media and potential customers, even those who hold an opposing view from yours. This merely gives you a chance to convince them otherwise.

65. It is possible to make your brochure and other sales materials so beautiful that the message about your business gets lost, so be careful when the copy seems to get buried.

66. Whenever you see an ad that you think is particularly effective or receive a direct mail piece that makes you get out your credit card, file it away for future use. When you prepare your next piece, you can take bits and pieces from the successful materials and incorporate them into your own.

67. To avoid clichés and frequently overused words in your marketing materials, use the thesaurus function in your word processing program.

68. Write all your marketing materials in a conversational style. Instead of writing copy on the computer, try reading it into a tape recorder and playing it back to see how it sounds . . . you'll immediately understand if it should be changed to strike the right tone.

69. If you plan to publish a newsletter to promote your business, make sure that it is aimed toward people who are already your customers. It'll make them feel as if they are part of your family as well as belonging to a larger, yet intimate, club of other customers who have shared the same experiences.

70. If your business is primarily directed at distinct groups of people or businesses, then be sure that your promotional materials reflect this. Make sure the name of each group—teachers or lawyers, for example—appears prominently on the front panel of the brochure or flyer.

71. You will get more business if the copy in your promotional materials focuses on the customer, not your business. If you can deliver a promise that will make your customer's life better, he or she will buy your product or service. This promise should be repeated several times in your copy—whether it's in a brochure or a radio advertisement.

72. To reinforce your customer-oriented message, make sure that you write all copy in the second person.

Designing Your Marketing Materials

73. You can add a touch of elegance and professionalism to your mailing pieces by using fancy preprinted papers available at relatively low cost from suppliers such as Paper Direct. It's much cheaper than multicolor printing, and it's a way to test out a new idea before you commit to thousands of new brochures.

74. Every sales letter that you send out should have something about it that physically stands out, whether it's bold-face letters, the occasional use of colored ink, or a personal note scrawled in the margin or as a P.S. But you should consider these to be the seasoning and not the main dish, because too many can quickly become overwhelming to the reader.

75. Highlighting pens and Post-It notes are great ways to make your promotional letters and brochures stand out in the minds of both customers and the media.

76. Your company logo needs to be clear and distinctive enough to be visible on a poster viewed from a long distance, or as a postage-stamp size on your literature. Before you make a final choice, look at your logo in a variety of contexts, colors, and sizes.

77. Pay close attention to the type of paper you choose for your promotional materials. Whether you decide to have textured paper, paper with a glossy finish, or a laid linen paper with a watermark, all convey a sense of the image you want to project for your business.

78. To make your posters stand out, consider designing them in the form of old-fashioned travel posters complete with a number of detailed, colorful photographs. Color copies are both striking and becoming more inexpensive every year.

79. Your logo and other signatures of your marketing campaign should be as simple as possible—and should reproduce well even in one color. The expense of using four-color art or photographs for logos may not be worth the investment.

80. When designing the text and art for your promotional materials, make sure that the design and typeface are consistent. Also make sure that there is enough white space in the piece. One of the most common mistakes that businesspeople make when designing their own marketing materials is to try to cram as many words into the space as possible. This usually ends up in chaos and confusion and finally potential customers skipping over to the next page because there are simply too many words. Of course, there are contrasting schools of thought regarding this idea; many designers who take a modernist approach to art believe in squeezing as many things onto the page as possible.

81. Your letterhead design should allow the majority of the space for the letter; however, you may include a list of your services and products to increase customers' awareness of the breadth of your business.

82. Illustrate your promotional materials with a picture of a person who is actually using and enjoying your product or service. People want to see what other people think of your product before they buy, and frequently a picture that shows this activity will do the trick.

83. Even the simplest graphic or illustration on the front of your promotional materials can capture a reader's attention in a way that no words can—a bull's-eye, arrows, or stars can have immediate impact.

84. If it's really important that a letter to a prospect looks like a letter from you, then make sure that the typeface and margins reflect this: use courier font and ragged-right margins for the best effect.

Your Brochure

85. Always include blurbs and quotes from articles and radio and TV shows in which you have been quoted or your business has been mentioned. Once you have had more than a few media appearances, it's not necessary to pull a direct quote from the story or show; instead, you can include a list of the publications and shows in which you have appeared, under the headline "As seen in . . ."

86. Before you introduce a new product, send out a teaser in the form of a brochure that shows the package design of the new product. Send it out two weeks before you introduce the item, and then when you do bring it to market, your customers will already be familiar with and looking for it.

87. When you plan to write the copy for your next brochure, marketing expert Barbara Brabec, author of the book *Homemade Money*, suggests that you specifically ask yourself what you want the brochure to accomplish: First, are you trying to get business from individuals by return mail with a check enclosed, or through an order on an 800 line with a credit card? Or are you trying to get the recipient to return an enclosed postage-paid reply card or other vehicle that says "Yes, send me detailed information by mail"? Or, are you mostly interested in getting an expression of interest so you can follow up with a personal sales call? Pick your angle and then make sure that the copy in your brochure clearly reflects this angle.

88. Consider producing your brochure as a spiral-bound booklet so customers will tend to keep it handy.

89. More companies are producing video brochures to tout the benefits of their businesses. The initial expense can be sizable, but video brochures tend to result in bigger returns due to the detailed information and images they present to customers.

90. Running out of brochures will cost you business. Always print more brochures and mailing pieces than you think you'll need. And if you do begin to run low, order more before you run out completely. Mark one box with "It's time to order more . . ."

91. Give your brochure a different theme each time you update it so the people who are on your regular mailing list will look forward to reading it: a continuing story, personal or family anecdotes, current events, whatever is most appropriate for the nature of your business and your customers.

92. If your business involves a leisure pursuit, you might consider investing in a video brochure that describes your business and specifically how it can help your customers to relax. Production costs don't need to be too high, but make it lush, plush, and irresistible. Keep in mind that your customers will be watching this at their leisure, so keep the pacing leisurely and the selling soft.

93. Ask a longtime customer to evaluate your brochure to determine if it realistically represents you and your business. Reward this customer with a dinner, a gift, or credit.

94. If you sell a product, design and write a brochure that will help to educate your customers about your product. For instance, health-food stores regularly provide brochures on vitamins and other nutritional supplements free of charge whether customers make a purchase or not. The more information you provide a customer about your product, the more likely she is to buy from you regularly.

95. Sometimes a homemade promotional piece is better for your business than a slick, four-color brochure. It all depends on the image you want to project, and the type of presentation to which *your* customers will respond.

Your Business Card

96. Be creative with your business card. Not only should you consider designing it with a vertical viewpoint and adding color, but you can also turn it into a miniature brochure by adding several panels to it so that people have to open it up to read it. You may also want to jazz it up by using two contrasting colors.

97. Your business cards can be tailored to different constituencies: depending upon the nature of your business, one card could target businesses, another individuals, etc.

98. The next time you need to get a new business card printed up, you should view it as a chance to make a statement. One bank vice president designed his business cards to resemble a miniature check. A phone card distributor used actual phone cards—with five minutes' worth of phone time included.

99. Premium companies offer magnetic business cards in the shape of a van, baseball, house, or whatever represents their business. Your customers will put these cards on the refrigerator, and not bury them in a drawer.

100. On one side of your business card, place the usual information. On the other side, print helpful information that your prospects can refer to again and again. For example, if you own a travel agency, print ten useful phrases in Spanish—or another language—on the back.

101. Make your business card more distinctive by designing it vertically.

102. Consider printing on both sides of your business cards. Many doctors, for instance, print their name, address, and phone number on one side and use the back side to jot down the time and date of the next appointment.

103. Business cards featuring your photo are particularly effective in fields that are people oriented, like real estate and other personal services.

104. Hand customers your business card to use as a frequent-buyer discount card. For example, a general store that gives one free gallon of milk after you buy ten can print spaces on the card where the storekeeper can keep track.

Other Ideas

105. If you operate a retail store in a busy tourist area, include photographs or line drawings of the more prominent tourist attractions in your area alongside pictures and information about your product or service to exhibit at the local Chamber of Commerce or tourist-information booth. You will become a destination of choice along with the usual tourist attractions, and people will connect you with being tourist friendly.

106. If you're using a banner, keep your message short— six or fewer words.

107. Calendars as a marketing tool never go out of style because your customers will be reminded about your business every day of the year. Make your calendar different and attractive; a watercolor painting of a lake won't cut it anymore, since there are so many humorous and beautiful calendars out there today. Humor helps, of course.

108. If you offer a wide variety of services and/or products to audiences that are pretty different from one another, you should have separate brochures aimed at each group. While much of the copy will be the same, the headlines, anecdotes, and perceived benefits may change to reflect the views and needs of each group.

109. Wholesaling to other businesses means you must help them sell your product. One way is to provide them with attractive merchandising and promotional material that will give their customers more information about your product.

110. Though they may seem old-fashioned, door hangers are an effective marketing tool for local businesses like restaurants, video stores, and dry cleaners. Print a price list or menu on each one, then distribute them around the neighborhood.

111. Market your business with a small advertising card that resembles either a driver's license or credit card. Especially if your business may be something that people will need in the future but not right now, handing out laminated cards in this style conveys a sense of value and permanence and will cause a lot of people to file it away instead of throwing it out.

112. Make up a credit-card-size calendar with your business information on one side and a full calendar (with your name at the top) on the other. It's a year's worth of advertising for only pennies.

113. One department store regularly sends out coupons with hidden discounts that are revealed when you rub off a seal with a coin, like some lottery tickets. You can promote the discount in the range of 10 to 50 percent, but the discount is only valid when they rub off the seal in the store right before the salesclerk rings up the purchase.

114. If you use an order form in your business, don't overlook this opportunity to promote your products or services. Not only should ordering be a streamlined process, but your order form can also promote specials and closeouts to customers. Victoria's Secret does this in almost every catalog they send out.

115. Make sure that the quality of all of your marketing materials is top-notch. If you use cheap paper or materials, this will reflect negatively on your business.

116. Consider your fax cover sheet to be a promotional tool. Include your company name, logo, and slogan at the very least. Include special limited offers and other late-breaking news in boxes at the bottom, but the cover sheet should not wholly detract from the message you're sending.

117. If you keep a pet on your premises, make it your mascot. Use it in your promotional materials—in the design or copy—to give your business a homey feel . . . there are a lot of animal lovers amongst your potential customers.

118. A video about your business can be a good promotion for potential customers. The script should provide just enough information but not overwhelm the visual message—in fact, your message should be clear even without the audio portion.

119. If you're on a tight budget, the cheapest way to get the word out is to use a simple one-sided flyer that you can tack on bulletin boards, put under windshield wipers, or even hand out to passersby.

GETTING PUBLICITY

Publicity in the form of media coverage is one of the most effective ways to market your business. Except for the cost of a press kit, postage, and phone calls, it costs you nothing but your time. In exchange, you'll receive stacks of press clips about your business and respect from your customers and competitors. Best of all, an appearance in the media is a tacit endorsement of your business; after all, you didn't have to pay to be mentioned. The reporter or producer thought highly enough of your business—and thought their audiences would like to know about you, too—to do a story about you.

So spend as much time as you can to get your business mentioned in the media. Think of how many potential customers you could reach.

Many a small-business person has been frightened away from seeking publicity about his business because he perceives any editor, writer, or reporter to be a temperamental, egotistical sort who believes he can play God because of a byline. True, these types do exist, but they are few and far between. It's more likely that you'll encounter media people who are genuinely interested in your business because of its newsworthiness and value to the community, or even the nation. We've already covered the aspects of getting publicity for your business, but contacting and then working with the media deserves a separate section because of the many nuances you'll encounter simply because you are dealing with other people who are working in a business that is as volatile as yours.

Press Kits

120. A press kit is the first thing you should have in your publicity arsenal. A press kit usually contains a cover letter, a press release, a copy of your brochure or other promotional material, a personal/professional biographical sheet, press clips, if you have them, and a photo or two all tucked into a folder. Why should you have a press kit? A press kit provides information about your business in a language that media people understand. This will make it more likely for a member of the media to decide to do a story on your business. A press kit provides a lot more information than the marketing materials, like brochures, that you provide to customers.

121. Most press kits are incomplete without at least one or two good-quality photographs that convey a little bit about your business. Photographs that are in focus and show easily identifiable objects are a good start, but in most cases you don't need a professional photographer for publishable pictures. If you run a people-oriented business, make sure that your press photos contain smiling people who are in the act of enjoying the services you offer.

122. When writing a press release, experiment with different typefaces and text sizes, in addition to using bold and italicized words when appropriate. Varying the text may ensure that your press release gets more than just a cursory once-over. However, too many type sizes and styles may be confusing and difficult to read. Instead, use italics and boldface for effective emphasis.

123. A cover letter should be brief, usually no more than a page. The first paragraph should consist of one sentence, and that line should be enticing and draw the reader in.

124. When writing your press release, it's okay to print on both sides of the page. In fact, in these environmentally conscious days, it's almost mandatory. While some marketers believe that some people can't be bothered enough to turn the paper over, others use this as a reason to restrict the release to one page.

125. Your press release should include a "release date." For timely material, it's "For Immediate Release." Otherwise, write "For Release at Will," which is appropriate for general news, etc.

126. If you've appeared on television, radio, or in the press a number of times, add a page to your press kit that lists all these appearances by media category. Be sure to include the dates and any other pertinent information about the programs or publications.

127. Don't let brightly colored paper stock make up for dull prose in your press release. Give the reader real information that she can use in news stories, columns, or roundups.

128. One press release does not necessarily fit every medium: the important information—the who, what, where, why, and how—goes into the body of the release. The introductory and closing paragraphs should address the needs of a particular market.

129. The bio sheet is essentially your résumé in prose format. This is important because sometimes an editor or producer may decide to do a story on your business based on your own personal history, so it helps if you play up something in your life that is either unusual or that follows current trends. In fact, it's a good idea to start right off the bat by making it your headline. For instance, if you've always dreamed of running your own business and struggled through an unsatisfying menial job for a number of years to save up the money, say so, and say it early on.

130. A press release should contain information that is timely and newsworthy. It should include the five Ws of newswriting—who, what, when, why, and where. It should be written in the form of news—with an enticing headline and points made in descending order of importance.

131. Send a press kit to a national producer or publication via overnight mail. Even if they don't know you, they will open an Express Mail envelope since it conveys a sense of urgency.

132. Sometimes, a visually striking photograph will do more to gain an editor's attention than a well-written press release. If you have such a photo, and it accurately conveys some aspect of your business, place it so that it's the first thing that an editor or producer will see when he opens up your press kit.

133. When building your press kit, be selective about the press clippings you include: they should be as current as possible featuring the publications with the largest circulation most prominently. You can also include radio and television interview tapes appropriately labeled with the date and time of the appearance and the call letters of the radio or TV station.

134. Don't be stingy with the press kits that you send out, even if you're on a tight budget. A well-placed kit—even with a long-shot prospect—can pay off handsomely with good coverage.

135. Try writing a personalized letter with a totally different angle for each editor and reporter on your list.

136. In these days of computerized mailings, a handwritten envelope may get more attention than a label that is obviously computer generated.

137. How can you make your press release stand out? Whether or not it's part of your press kit, printing it on parchment paper, printing it in calligraphy or an unusual typeface, or even printing it on a brown paper bag will help it stand out.

138. Whenever you write to the press, it sometimes helps to suggest three different story ideas and set them apart by using boldface, bullets, and plenty of white space around them to make them stand out. Tell the producer or editor about the benefits of your business, and then have a stable of experienced, happy users who are willing to talk about their experience with your business.

139. Many marketing experts will tell you that you're wasting your money if you neglect to personalize the cover letters you send out to the media in your press kit. However, a detailed and informative letter directed to Dear Editor can be effective (and besides, the time it takes to personalize each letter in a media mailing could be overwhelming). If you wish to add a personalized touch, write a short note in pen at the bottom of the letter.

140. Whenever a news story hits with information that casts a negative light on your business, take action by creating a press release that shows the other side of the story.

141. Photos are an important part of your press kit. Though a newspaper will frequently send a photographer to take a picture to accompany a story about you and your business, some of the smaller papers don't have the budget or the time, and they'll usually publish whatever you send them. A five-by-seven or eight-by-ten glossy black-and-white photograph—usually a picture of you doing whatever you do at your business—will do. Don't send color prints or slides unless they're specifically requested.

142. Some entrepreneurs enclose a reply card in their press kits that media people can fill out and return to let them know if they're interested in continuing to receive press kits. This can help to keep your media mailing list clean and invite response.

143. The next time you write a press release, angle it so that it tells about you, the expert behind the business, and not just about the business. Members of the media are always looking for experts to profile and to use as their sources.

144. Follow the example of direct mail companies and put a teaser on the envelope you use to send out a press kit. Make it an irresistible pitch and watch your PR placements increase.

145. If you don't consider yourself to be a writer, try this: hire a freelance writer or publicist to create a bare-bones publicity kit, with cover letter, press release, and perhaps a question-and-answer sheet, and to supply you with names of 100 appropriate press contacts. Then send the kits out on your stationery and make the follow-up calls yourself. This way, you'll get a professionally written press kit at a greatly reduced rate.

146. To make your press kit stand out, focus on the package it comes in. The outside envelopes and folders can be color-matched to your logo, or you can choose the colors of a specific holiday that revolves around the topic of the press kit. A distinctive color or design will alert your regular contacts of a package from you.

147. No matter what type of marketing piece you are planning, always try to include a little graphic with the text, whether it's just a geometrical shape or a photo or drawing that involves your business in some way. There are plenty of clip art programs out there on the market today that can provide you with hundreds and even thousands of choices.

148. Watch your tone when sending letters and other materials to the media; play it safe and address reporters and editors with "Mr." or "Ms." in the salutation. One editor gently chastises writers who address her by her first name, both on the phone and in letters, telling them that she prefers to be addressed with a title by people she doesn't know.

149. When choosing a basic color for the stationery that goes in your press kit, make sure that the color you choose matches the product or service you are selling. For instance, an ice company would naturally choose blue whereas a landscaper would select green. So make sure that the color you choose matches your intentions.

150. In the eyes of some editors, the more homegrown your press materials appear, the more likely they are to read your press releases. Avoid slick, expensive-looking paper and folders.

Selecting Your Angle

151. Your press materials should tell how your business will help the editors and readers improve their lives in some way, whether it's to save time or to help them relax.

152. Any written materials you send out to the press should be timely: explain why you're writing to the editor at this particular time, whether it is to alert the media to a special event or to provide them with an introduction to your new business.

153. Conduct a survey of your customers to find out what they really think of your business, as well as your industry as a whole. Then take the information, assemble it into a press release, and send it out to the media to promote your business in a very newsworthy fashion.

154. Many publications devote space to new products and services. This is one of the easiest ways to see print and to establish contact with an editor at that publication for future, more in-depth stories.

155. If you can present your business as one way to provide a solution to a current problem—from obesity to illiteracy to crime—you'll increase your chances for good placement in media.

156. If you regard your business as a good place for mothers and fathers to work, be sure to promote this fact in separate press releases. Workplace issues are very important in the media, and if you make a big deal of the fact that your company is enlightened about the welfare of your employees, the press will be more likely to mention your company.

157. If you regularly work out co-op advertising deals with your suppliers, turn it into news by sending a note about it to the media when a supplier introduces a brand-new product at your store.

158. Many publications plan up to a year ahead for seasonal articles. A seasonal angle may actually improve your chances of getting placement, since editors are always looking for new twists on the usual stories.

159. Whenever you do something that's the least bit out of the ordinary for your industry, send out a press release to announce it to the media.

160. What is the human-interest element of the story you are proposing to an editor or producer? Has your product changed someone's life or made an impact on the way an industry does business? Is it part of a consumer trend, or does it anticipate one? The stories that make the news are, after all, stories about what people are doing.

Choosing Your Media Contacts

161. Anyone you know who works at a newspaper, magazine, TV or radio station—even in a service department—

can be your first contact with the world of public relations. Even the advertising rep can be a good conduit to the editorial departments. Also, a contact at a radio station, for instance, may be your best introduction to other media— television, newspapers, or magazines . . . media circles are small and are not always competitive.

162. Don't automatically discount local cable and public-access TV shows. They do tend to have a loyal audience of regulars. Also, the shows are frequently repeated numerous times over the course of a week.

163. If the publications that you would most like your business to appear in publish regional sections, approach the editors of these sections first. For instance, *Good Housekeeping* publishes seven different regional sections, *Travel & Leisure* and the *New York Times* publish a number of regional editions. The editorial material in these sections features local people in businesses, and sometimes the editors of these regional sections are really scraping for material. In these media, the local angle helps to establish what you and your business are doing to make your community a better place in which to live, etc.

164. Look to the hometown media in the place you grew up to place a "Native Son (or Daughter) Does Good" article.

165. Next time you're at the bookstore, check out the latest books that have been published on the subject of your business. Send a letter to the author in care of the publisher including a press kit about your business and any other pertinent information that ties it in with their new book. Most writers tend to concentrate on the same subject areas, so making contact with the author of this book may well guarantee you a place in her next book.

166. The editorial offices at some publications and TV and radio stations are revolving doors, which means that the producer that you spoke to last week may no longer be there this week. Therefore, it's important to keep your list updated to avoid wasting time and money. Hire a college student or intern to do the job.

167. To decide whom to contact at a publication, check the name of the editor on the masthead or the staff writer. Never contact the editor in chief of a large and/or frequent publication, since he will be far too busy to respond to you. The managing editor or an associate editor in charge of a specific department is a much better choice.

168. When drawing up your media list, don't forget about the publications from corporations and local non-profit organizations.

169. If you feel that your public relations campaign is getting a bit unwieldy, cut it down to a select, more manageable group of 50 targeted publications and radio and TV stations. When there are 950 newspapers and 12,000 magazines in existence, some businesses are deciding to target only a few and then hammer away at them.

170. Know your media. When you approach an editor with a story idea, you should know the range of stories—and ads—that have appeared in the magazine during the past year. Tailoring your pitch to the specific magazine will impress an editor and increase your chances of placement.

171. Good publicity can begin in the most unlikely places. For instance, a country inn sent a note to an editor at *Home Office Computing* to explain how they turned their business around in five years by using computers. The magazine included the inn in a feature they were planning on business turnarounds, which, in turn, caught the attention of a business editor at the Sunday *New York Times*. The *Times* wrote a brief article about these same innkeepers a few months later. The *Times* article prompted a response from *Country Home*, which eventually ran a feature on the inn.

172. Instead of contacting one of the editors at a particular publication, write to the freelance writers and contributing editors who are listed on the masthead, in care of the magazine, which will pass it along. Staff writers frequently are given assignments based on ideas that are generated in-house; freelancers are usually responsible for coming up with their own ideas, so if you provide them with a salable idea, they may cover it for more than one publication.

173. If you're unsure about to whom to send your press release, send it to a number of different staffers at the same publication or station. Sometimes it helps to hit as many people at a particular publication as possible to increase your chances of exposure.

174. Some journalists belong to associations that specialize in particular fields; e.g., sports, travel, food, etc. Contact the association relevant to your business to acquire a list of writers in your area if they make such names available or for information on how to best work with these members. Check the *Directory of Associations* for pertinent groups.

175. There are several valuable newsletters that list what editors, producers, and writers from radio, TV, magazines, and newspapers are looking for; for example, *Party Line*, a two-page weekly newsletter that includes a real mix of media who are actively looking for sources. To request a sample copy and to get subscription information, send a letter to Party Line, 35 Sutton Place, New York, NY, 10022; or call 212-755-3487.

176. If you're trying to decide which type of media to pursue for the best results, go for the magazines first, then newspapers, then TV, and radio last. Many entrepreneurs find that magazines give them the best overall response since they tend to hang around longer. Newspapers can also pull in the orders, although the coverage is usually over and done with within a week.

Pursuing the Press

177. Before you send anything to the media, make sure that the contact is still current. Don't just send it to the

Editorial Department or to a producer without attaching a specific name to it. Addressing a mailing to "To Whom It May Concern" or "Current Resident" will guarantee its being consigned quickly to the wastebasket.

178. Frequently, journalists are like cattle. They won't cover a story unless somebody else has done it first. But contrary to popular belief, it's not difficult to get press—in many cases, all you have to do is ask for it. If you're new in town, or if you've done something new for your business, that's news and you should contact a reporter about it even if you haven't been written up in the past. Try the business editor at your local daily, or the features editor at your local community weekly paper for a start.

179. Even if a reporter just calls for a brochure, you should add them to the media list and regularly send out personalized notes about new features or programs that concern your business.

180. Most people dream of seeing their names in headlines in the *New York Times*. It's rare to get a credit in a paper of record in the early years of your business, but you'll improve your chances if you know something about how to work your way up the ladder. First contact your state Associated Press bureau, or the state bureau of the nearest large newspaper. Once you see ink in these sections, then find out who the stringer or bureau chief for the *New York Times* is in your area, and then send that person information about your business, along with any clips.

181. Invite a member of the press to spend a few hours in your shoes, exposing her to all the ups and downs of your business.

182. Once a reporter or a producer in one department or at one particular show declines to do a story on you or your company, immediately call another department editor or TV show at the same station. For instance, your book on gardening may not get reviewed in the book section but could be a good feature piece for the gardening editor.

183. Follow up your press kit mailing with a personal letter from you every two or three months in which you mention some of your unusual promotions as well as the more interesting tidbits about your business and your industry. After sending the first couple of letters, follow them up with a brief phone call just to make voice contact. If you don't get the kind of reception you'd hoped for, try contacting another editor or producer at the same place.

184. Some publicity professionals suggest that the best way not only to keep your name out there but also to keep in practice is to book yourself onto at least one radio show each day.

185. Make sure that the media know how to contact you—or a member of your staff—twenty-four hours a day.

186. Syndicated columnists who cover very specialized fields are often overlooked by small-business owners. Of course, everybody would like their business to be mentioned in Dear Abby, but you have a much better chance of placement by approaching a columnist—either local or national—who specializes in your field. For instance, a computer store that has come up with a unique way of informing previous customers about the ease of upgrading their systems could approach both a local computer columnist as well as a national one. Offer to give readers more information over an 800 number or through the mail.

187. Be gracious whenever a reporter or producer goes to the trouble to quote you in a story or to mention your business. Reporters frequently write stories that are longer than required; this means that more often than not, the story will be cut, which can result in the quotes of sources being cut or eliminated entirely. Write a thank-you note anyway; the reporter will then tend to keep you in mind for future stories.

188. With some editors, the way to their hearts is definitely through their stomachs. Some marketers report that sending food with their press kits is the most effective way to get ink, even if the food is totally unrelated to the product.

189. Before you send out any correspondence to the media, make sure you double-check the spelling and title of the editor's or producer's name. This will help prevent unnecessary mailings and embarrassment.

190. Even if you think your story is a perfect one for a particular publication or show, let the reporter or editor come to that conclusion. Otherwise, it's a good bet that if you demand that your business be covered editors and producers will put you on a blacklist.

191. If one of the two newspapers in your town has written up your business, wait a while until you approach the second paper. Your pitch to the second paper should be unique, such as a seasonal story or a special event you're planning.

192. If you discover that a new reporter is covering your beat at a local newspaper, offer to serve as an initial contact as well as a sounding board he can call to ask stupid questions.

193. If you pitch an idea to one reporter and she turns you down, ask for the name of another reporter or editor who might be more appropriate. Then use the first reporter's name when contacting the next one.

194. If you're finding it difficult to get the attention of a particular editor or reporter, invite him to lunch or even breakfast at a good restaurant to break the ice. Make sure that you tell him that you have a bit of important information to give him when you meet.

195. Once you've made initial contact with an editor or producer and have talked briefly over the phone, offer to make a special trip to drop off additional information in person. This way, the media person has a face to connect to the press kit and may even pull you aside to ask you some questions as long as you're there.

196. One of the best ways to endear yourself to a member of the media is to get a copy of their upcoming editorial calendar and then slant your topic to a particular themed issue. You can request the annual editorial calendars that most magazines and many newspapers create.

197. One way that you can increase your chances of successful placement is to promise the editor or reporter an exclusive. Tell her you're going to her first with the story because you thought that she would be the best person to break the story. Don't overdo the flattery, however; throw out just enough. And make sure that you really have a story that is worth an exclusive, or else you'll risk alienating the media.

198. Should you use faxes or regular mail to contact members of the media? If it's unsolicited, I would rely on regular mail. Editors and producers today seem to be making themselves more and more inaccessible because the number of methods that are used to reach them have increased. Once upon a time, there was mail and the telephone. Then came messenger services, fax machines, and electronic mail; this latter method of communication, however, is rapidly turning into a media person's favored method of communication. Why? It's simple to respond.

199. Fax broadcasting can be quite effective when you need to get late-breaking news about your company to the media. While some reporters and editors don't care to receive fax press releases from companies they're not familiar with, they probably won't mind if it means that they are able to scoop their rivals. To locate a database of fax numbers for the media, contact Ad-Lib Publications at 800-669-0773.

200. Whenever a reporter or producer has written up your business, even in passing, write them a thank-you note. In the note, offer to continue to serve as a resource in the future.

201. Whenever a story about your business has appeared in the national media, or a prominent local or regional publication or show, make a copy of it and send it to your wish list of media people. This usually works best when you send the mention to producers and editors you may have already approached. Attach a simple, handwritten note—"Thought you'd be interested in this"—and your business card.

202. Most editors will not write you up the first time they hear of you. A gentle, consistent barrage of mailings is necessary to keep your name in front of an editor. First you send a press kit. A month or two later, you follow it up with a personal letter inviting the editor to see what you're all about. Then, perhaps a personal visit to the editor's office. In time, your steady, persistent efforts should bear fruit.

Follow-up Calls to the Media

203. When making follow-up calls to the media, don't write up a phone script. You'll sound more natural, and therefore be more effective, if you just learn to wing it, relying on your smarts instead of a canned package.

204. If you don't have a lot of time to do follow-up calls, focus on those media that you most like to be mentioned in.

205. When doing follow-up calls to the media, if you don't have a lot of time, call only the largest media; some of the editors and producers here get so many press releases and press kits that they don't even look at most of them. In this case, a phone call may be your best bet.

206. Whenever you call a media person to find out information before you send anything or to follow up on materials that you did send, the first thing you should do is ask if this is a good time for him to talk. He might be under deadline or he might have just had a fight with his boss. Then quickly ask your question or say your piece and let it go. Gauge by the tone of their voice whether you should say anything else.

207. A follow-up call to your press mailing can effectively increase your chances of getting an interview or review. While you are speaking to an editor or producer, you can elaborate on some aspects of your business that are noted only briefly in the press kit. She, in turn, might have a couple of questions, even though the answers may appear in the press kit, it's better off if she hears them directly from you.

208. If, when making a follow-up call to your press release, you have to leave a message, be sure to call back. Chances are that the message either won't get to the intended person, or it will be ignored. Find out when your contact will be available and call him back then.

209. Follow-up calls require time and patience. It takes a few calls in a row to get into a rhythm and be able to speak with confidence and clarity, so you may want to make those first calls to media people you already know.

Press Conferences and Media Events

210. Once you schedule a press conference, arrange for someone to transcribe a tape of the proceedings. After the conference, check the list of media people who didn't show up at the event, and send them a transcript of the conference along with other pertinent information.

211. When planning a press conference, be sure that is the best way to provide information to reporters and wouldn't be better handled through a press release or a phone call. The reason? The press may show up in force the first time that you announce a press conference, but if it doesn't provide them with anything newsworthy or controversial, the next time you hold a conference, you'll be lucky if any of them show up. If in doubt, call a media person whom you are close to and ask her opinion before you even schedule a press conference.

212. If you run the type of business in which it's important that the premises be so clean that you could eat off the floor, then stage a publicity stunt where you do just that.

213. When planning your next publicity stunt, think in extremes. A small specialty foods company in Vermont called Uncle Dave's Kitchen once made the biggest Bloody Mary in the United States—350 gallons—using their own mix. This resulted in favorable write-ups in the *Boston Globe*, the *New York Times*, and the *Wall Street Journal*.

214. Have a contest where your customers and potential customers can enter something that is near and dear to their hearts, from an arts-and-craft project to a car, even a favorite recipe.

215. Hold a contest to name your new mascot or another tangible and catchy aspect of your business.

216. To market your business to parents, invite local schoolchildren to paint your store windows with a seasonal mural.

217. If you have a business where customers can come to you, plan a springtime Clean Sweep sale to clear out inventory and get some media attention, besides. Offer each customer who brings in a broom 20 percent off his total purchase, and provide valet broom parking outside your shop. To get media attention, send a miniature broom with a press kit and all the details about the sale to your local media.

218. Consider holding a press conference when you're introducing something new to the market. Make sure that you have an important news hook that will attract the media.

219. If you want to invite the media to a function that is important to your business but wouldn't be considered news—like introducing a new line or opening a new store—consider holding a press party instead. At one of these functions, the main attraction is the party, and there's rarely a formal question-and-answer session as is the case at a press conference. Be sure to hand out press kits at the end of the party as the media are leaving the room, and see if you can't hold the party at an unusual venue; for one business, an empty baseball stadium worked like a charm.

In Print/On the Air

220. In this day of shock jocks like Howard Stern, it's possible that you will get booked on a radio talk show where the host's priority is to insult his guests. If your interview starts to veer off in this direction, stay calm, and stick to the points of the interview. Above all, don't yell back and don't be confrontational—even though that is what the host and producers are looking for.

221. When doing a radio talk show outside your home turf, try to review the news in that area before you do the show. It will help tremendously if you are able to tie in your product or service with a newsworthy event in that town.

222. Whenever you do a radio phone interview, use one of those phone headsets. This will help prevent you from nervously handling the phone during the interview; these noises will be magnified on a radio broadcast.

223. Even though you're the interviewee, try to take the lead. Don't just answer yes or no, and be sure to give an answer that will lead to another question, preferably one that's different from the one the interviewer had in mind. For instance, answer the question, and then add a salient point that the interviewer may not know about. This makes for more interesting and usually longer interviews.

224. Free samples can be your least expensive and best way to publicize your business in the media. A company called Find People Fast performs complimentary searches for people who call in on live radio talk shows on which the company appears. This "free" advertising success generates thousands of inquiries from paying customers each year.

225. On radio call-in shows, often the questions that the callers ask will have nothing to do with your subject. You should make sure to keep the subject coming back to you, so thank the caller for his question, answer it in the best and briefest way you can, then bring up a point that hasn't been addressed on the show.

226. If you live in a town with a small radio station, you might consider offering to host a weekly talk show where you can interview local people as well as promote your own business. Janine Weins, who runs Your Idea bookstore in Lebanon, New Hampshire, does just that. She hosts a live one-hour morning radio talk show direct from the store Monday through Friday; she interviews people on a wide variety of topics and, whenever possible, tells listeners about related books on that day's topic that they can find in her store.

227. A review of your product or service in the media is only one step toward generating sales. Feature articles that focus on your business and your experience in launching your company bring in far more sales than product reviews, which often get buried in the back of a publication.

228. If a glowing feature article has been written about your business, turn it into a brochure by reprinting it in its entirety so that it forms the interior of your brochure. In the exterior of the brochure, assuming that it has three panels, include the cover, a mailing panel, and a panel that lists contact information, pricing, etc.

229. While doing radio talk shows, make sure you write down the name of the host, and then use his or her name liberally throughout the interview. (One time, I mistakenly wrote down the name of the producer and ended up referring to the host by another name on the air.)

230. If you're looking to secure a deal with a major distributor, and are coming up against brick walls, try to get your product and company booked on some regional talk shows on radio or TV. Keep track of the number of orders you fill as a result of these appearances, then send a tape of the appearance with the sales figures to the distributors. One small specialty food producer banged on the door of a distributor for four years without luck. One day, she was quoted in the *Wall Street Journal*; the next day, four distributors were knocking on her door.

231. One great way to get yourself a regular spot on a radio station to promote your business is by supplying the station with a weekly update on news in your area. For instance, a financial services firm reports about the stock market results every day in a three-minute report. A ski resort reports on snow conditions not only at its own slopes but at other ski areas as well. Always be sure to sign off with your name and the name of your business at the end of the broadcast.

232. You can write a service article on a subject in your field that includes giving advice through anecdotes or tips for newspapers or magazines. When you do this free of charge, you'll get compensated through a blurb at the end of each article that contains information about how to get in touch with you and about your products and/or services. You might even negotiate to receive a free ad in the same issue that the column appears in.

233. Write op-ed articles for your local newspaper. A bio line at the end of each article that explains who you are and why this subject is pertinent to you is almost a rule of thumb in op-ed pieces. You don't have to be a professional writer to get published either. Says Michelle West, a small Canadian publisher, "You need only three things to get published: You need to be able to write reasonably well; you need to learn the skills necessary to market what you produce; and you need the self-confidence and courage to go after what you want."

234. If you regularly do phone-in radio shows, work hard to become more entertaining by sharpening your responses to the interviewers' frequently predictable questions. This will help make you more entertaining and therefore a better guest, not to mention increasing your business revenues.

235. Think of a radio or TV show as if you are on a job interview. Think of the important points you want to make, be on your best behavior, and look the interviewer in the eye if you're on TV.

236. When a reporter calls to say that she is planning to mention your business as a blurb in the next issue, keep in mind that if you make a favorable impression on her, this blurb may actually grow into a feature article as you continue to talk. So be helpful whenever you talk to members of the media and always give them more information than they need. There's a good chance that they'll come back to you in the future.

237. When you appear on a TV talk show, one of the most important things you have to keep in mind is your body language. Fidgeting and lack of eye contact with your host can easily distract the viewer from the point you're trying to make.

238. Whenever doing a radio phone interview from your home or office, stand instead of sitting.

239. Whenever a photographer takes your picture for a newspaper or magazine, be sure to wear a T-shirt, sweatshirt, or cap that clearly shows the name of your business. Many times, contact information will be left out of an article for space reasons, so you'll be covered with this visual reminder.

240. Whenever you do a phone interview on a talk show, try to arrange with the producer in advance to give away something from your business. Whether it's a product such as a free CD, a meal in a restaurant, or a car wash, this will ensure that your business gets even more exposure on the radio station.

241. Whenever you plan a trip out of your area, and you have a product or service that you market on a nationwide basis, make up a list of the radio stations, TV stations, and newspapers in the major towns along the way. The week before you leave for your trip, send them information to inform them that you'll be passing through and ask to schedule a show.

242. Write a column in your local weekly newspaper about some aspect of area life. Don't look at the column as a blatant way to promote your business, because that will be a turnoff to readers. Instead, you can bring your experience as a businessperson into play every so often, while you concentrate more on the positive qualities of your area that you share with your readers.

Other Ideas

243. For your business, find a compelling related object to hand-deliver to your most desired media contacts, and then do it.

244. If it's appropriate, try to get your product or service featured as a prize on a local or national game show. This is an effective and fun way to build exposure for your company.

245. If you or one of your employees has written an article about some aspect of your business that has appeared in a local or national publication, post a blowup of it at the entrance of your business. Send it to your 100 best customers.

246. If you're selling a product, and it's not bigger than a breadbox, it's a good idea to enclose a sample of it with the press kit, or send it out a week after you've sent out the press kit. For an editor or producer, this is one of the best parts of being a member of the media: all those free samples. Inevitably, the most popular items always seem to find their way into the magazine or newspaper or on the air.

247. You might consider hiring a novice PR consultant and offer incentives for results in lieu of a high flat fee. Some business owners say that novices are better than experts; although they don't have the contacts, they also don't have a lot of preconceived notions about what's right and what's wrong.

248. One overlooked way to get publicity for your business is to call in to a live radio talk show that invites listener feedback. Mention your expertise at the beginning and be sure to make a point or give your opinion, and not just mention your business. Other callers may call in to ask how they can get in touch with you, and the show's producer may invite you back to be a guest on the show.

249. One thing you should do when designing publicity campaigns is to borrow liberally from other industries. For instance, publishers send their authors out on book tours. Why can't a software company send a team of programmers out on tour too when a new program comes out?

250. One somewhat risky trick that some publicists use to promote a business is to leave some unique and tantalizing information out of a press release. Then, when the publicist calls to follow up on the release, she can tell the reporter about what was left out, which may be all it takes for the reporter to decide to do a story.

251. An interview with a media person can be planned in advance so that you can make notes about particular issues you want to mention during the interview. The more prepared you are, the better.

252. One author who is extremely effective at getting his work written up in the media has a secret weapon: an extensive rubber stamp collection. When he sends out press mailings, he stamps the envelopes with an appropriate image, in colored ink.

253. News USA at (202) 682-2400, or Metro Creative Graphics at (212) 947-5100 are two agencies that will write a newspaper-oriented article about a business, typeset it, (include a picture if necessary), and syndicate it to more than ten thousand newspapers across the country, mostly small weeklies. The benefit to the newspapers is that the articles are camera-ready and they only have to pay a small fee to the syndicate. The disadvantage is that they probably won't contain any local news, which will make a newspaper more reluctant to use them.

254. Writing a letter to the editor is a good way to promote your business. You can respond to a recent article, citing your experience with your business to underscore the point you're making. Then invite readers to contact you for more information. Many publications will print the name and full address of their letter writers.

255. Include a preprinted Rolodex card listing your name, address, and other contact information with your press materials. On the tab of the card, include your area of specialty to enable a reporter to use you as a source in future stories on the topic. You may also choose to hand your Rolodex card out to past, present, and future customers.

256. Whenever you do something new for your business, contact the alumnae/i association at any of the schools you've ever attended.

257. Whenever you have some news to promote about your business, contact the trade associations that you belong to to inform them of the news.

DIRECT MAIL

Most people refer to what can be a very effective form of marketing as "junk mail," but the truth is that as Americans' lives become increasingly busy and complex, men, women, and children will be more likely to respond to an offer that they receive in the mail, whether it's for a well-earned vacation or a case of dog food.

The secret to effective direct mail selling is first to select a mailing list that will "pull"—in direct marketing parlance—and then to tinker with your sales letter, order form, even the color of the envelope you use until you find the combination that brings in the best response. In this way, entrepreneurs who use direct mail to do even a small percentage of their marketing will discover that this form of marketing is akin to a game of golf: they know they can always score higher, so they never stop obsessing over it. In the case of direct mail, however, a little obsession is a good thing.

How to Write a Direct Mail Piece That Sells

258. If you've received a rave review of your product or service from a well-known publication or respected person, use one of the more laudatory blurbs in your direct mail letter.

259. Don't waste your direct mail budget on image advertising; i.e., simply introducing your product or service. The most effective direct mail advertising makes the potential customer a great offer or irresistible promise.

260. Increase your response rate with a delayed billing option. This can be a time-consuming and expensive offer for you; however, given delinquent customers, it's much easier and safer just to accept credit card orders.

261. Send out articles that have appeared about your business with brochures to all potential customers. This can impress some people so that they become regular customers.

262. When your business is written up in the press, send the articles to your list of current customers and offer them a special deal to help you celebrate your appearance in the publication.

263. Boost the response to your mailing by stressing the exclusivity of your product or service. If what you're selling isn't available in stores or to the general public, your response rate should go up as a result.

264. When in doubt, write more. Direct response experts report that the longer the cover letter, the higher the response rate. The more information you can provide a potential customer, the more confident he will feel sending money to a company with which he probably hasn't done business before.

265. When writing a direct mail letter, be as specific in the salutation as you can. For instance, don't just write "Dear Reader." Instead, direct the letter to the type of person to whom you are sending the package; for example, "Dear Cat Lover" or "Dear Brooklyn Entrepreneur."

266. When writing your direct mail order, don't just state a problem; always explain why that problem isn't going to disappear—not without your company, that is.

267. In addition, be specific about the negative effects that the reader will experience if she doesn't take advantage of your order *right now*.

268. When composing your next sales letter, try writing the last paragraph first. It should be the P.S. Some studies have shown that after the first paragraph, many readers skim the rest of the letter and skip to the P.S. to see what the offer is about in a nutshell.

269. Test your offer by changing some aspect of your offer so that you're essentially sending out a number of different mailing pieces to the same list. For instance, change the type of free item you send to people who respond. This is an effort to help you test which offer brings in the greatest response. Sometimes, something as innocuous as adding more white space in the margin will help boost response. As direct marketing pros say, "Test, test, test."

270. In your direct mail letters, always state the obvious. Never assume what your reader knows, no matter how basic the information. If you're thinking "But everybody knows that," you're giving more credit than is necessarily due.

271. Put an expiration date on every offer you make. This will result in a burst of orders in the beginning and also near the deadline. A four- to six-week deadline has been proven to be most effective.

272. When your direct mail letter runs longer than a page, be sure to add a note at the bottom of the first page in parentheses that reads either "more" or "please turn the page."

273. Your order form should spell out in plain English the details of your offer. When in doubt, write for the lowest common denominator.

274. When you write your order form or reply card, it's very important that you restate the offer that you described in detail in the cover letter. And don't forget to place your phone number and mailing address on the order form as well.

How to Design a Direct Mail Piece That Sells

275. If you can include something in your direct mail package that gets the reader involved, you should do it. Publishers Clearing House is famous for enclosing many involvement tools in each of its mailings—from cards where you rub off a gray bar to see if you're a winner, to peeling off and sticking on a gold coin stamp, to tearing open a miniature envelope. These devices have been shown to increase the response.

276. Get attention in a direct mail letter by using the effect of a highlighter pen to draw attention to salient points.

277. If you decide to send your direct mail package bulk rate, try to use those bulk rate postage stamps instead of an indicia that screams that it's a direct mail solicitation. More and more companies are choosing this route as more and more North Americans get totally buried by bulk mailings.

278. If you lease a postage meter for your business, there's usually space on the stamp where you can put a message from your business. Use the space creatively with an intriguing message that changes periodically—a suitable proverb or observation that's even tangentially related to your business can be appropriate.

279. In your direct mail letter, highlight the most important parts of the letter by printing them in another color.

Red tends to be the most effective second color in a direct mail letter, but don't overdo it or it will lose its intended impact.

280. In your next mailing package, print the order form in green to resemble a dollar bill that represents the top end of the amount that customers could save with you if they take advantage of your offer. Make sure that the first sentence that appears on this bill is set in the largest typeface on the paper and powerfully restates your irresistible offer.

281. Your company, address, and 800 number should appear on every piece in your mailing, including the envelope. Even if the customer has lost the order form or main sales letter, it's still possible to place an order with you.

282. Direct mail pieces usually include a teaser on the outside envelope. You may want to try sending yours in a plain white envelope that shows nothing but your return address, the addressee's address, and a 32-cent stamp. This approach can be even more effective if you leave the name of your business off your return address.

283. Should you include a photograph of the product you're selling in a direct mail piece? Many times this is not necessary, but if the majority of your sales depends on your customers' ability to see the product clearly, you should opt for a photo.

284. Aside from the structure and content of the cover letter, the design of the outside of the envelope of your direct mail package is probably the most hotly debated subject among direct marketing professionals. Many entrepreneurs find that simple works best: this means put your return address in the upper left-hand corner and include a teaser of some kind in the lower left. This brief phrase should entice the recipient to open up the envelope, which is sometimes a great challenge, especially if you send your package bulk rate.

285. The most commonly used—and the most effective—colors used in direct mail pieces are black ink for the typeface and red for headlines, graphics, or standouts.

286. When you send out mailings to both current and potential customers, every so often you should try to use as many stamps on the envelope as possible. This will create a sense of curiosity about your business, since it shows that you do business differently from others. However, as this method can be expensive in terms of the labor required to produce the mailings, you may want to restrict this idea to smaller mailings.

Mailing Lists

287. Whenever you rent a mailing list, make sure that you find out if the names on the list are people who have inquired about a product that's similar to yours or have actually bought a product through direct sales that is similar to yours. Obviously, the list of bona fide buyers is more valuable—and will cost more to rent—than a list of people who have merely asked for information about products or services in your field.

288. Barter your house mailing list for another list from a business that is not in direct competition with you. Although there may be some overlap with your own house list, this is an inexpensive way to conduct a direct mailing campaign.

289. How often do you clean your in-house mailing list? About 20 percent of the population changes addresses every year, so if you're not keeping up with them, you're wasting time and money. Turn your brochure and other marketing materials into a self-mailer with a bulk mail indicia with address correction requested under your return address.

290. If you plan to rent out your in-house mailing list to get some additional revenue, make sure that your customers know what you are doing. In fact, it's always good to give them the option of checking off a box in your next mailing where they can tell you that they don't want you to sell or rent their names. If they discover that you included their names on your rented list without their consent, it's possible that this may alienate them from your business in the future.

291. If you really want to get on the good side of the customers on your mailing list, promise them that you won't rent or sell their names to any other company. They know you can make money from doing so and will be impressed by your consideration and integrity.

292. If you rent a mailing list from a broker, the minimum number of names you'll probably have to rent is 5,000. It's perfectly okay to mail to 1,000 at a time (which you can target by location or other criteria); however, you should keep in mind that the longer you wait before you mail, the more likely it is that some of your addresses will become outdated.

293. Be sure to clean your in-house mailing list frequently. If you do, you will save money and increase your rate of response.

Getting Creative with Direct Mail

294. Invoke the name of a famous historical figure for your direct mail offer and then design your entire piece around it. For example, Johnny Appleseed or Betsy Ross or George Washington all create images of righteous, good Americans with accompanying graphics. Go all out to attract your customers.

295. Go to your post office and buy up some of the more unusual commemorative stamps that are being produced today. Not long ago, there was a series of stamps that saluted old cartoons including Andy Capp and the Yellow Kid. Using some of these more unusual stamps will encourage your prospects to open up your piece of mail.

296. Encourage your respondents to save some time by asking them to tape their business card to the order form instead of filling it out. This will also help give you more information about each respondent.

297. For a great attention-getter, put your direct mail offer—or a free sample—inside a can. Contact Vantec, a packager that provides this service, at (800) 475-0660 for more information.

298. One way to attract a lot of attention to your direct mail piece is to enclose an item that is universally known but unrelated to your offer. For instance, one company enclosed a pack of Juicy Fruit chewing gum in each mailing, "for you to enjoy while you browse through our offerings."

299. Mail a series of postcards. The messages can be individual teasers or feature only part of your message on each card. Don't forget to include your name and address in small print on each card. Your final mailing should probably include the whole message (or you can ask consumers to collect all the cards for a gift or discount).

300. If you run a business where there is a time lag between the customer's initial commitment and the time when the service is to be used—such as a bed-and-breakfast—it's a good idea to send a letter immediately after the initial contact. A brief, personal note of confirmation will go a long way toward cementing your long-term relationship with your customer.

301. One great way to attract attention is to Express Mail a direct mail package to a new customer. With quantities over 500 pieces, the express delivery companies will come down on their standard prices.

302. An audiotape can be an inexpensive way to keep in touch with major customers—it's like a personal visit from you that will keep customers abreast of what's happening in your company. Make it fun with lots of sound effects, and sign off with a promise of another one later that year. It will give your customers something to look forward to. By its very nature, direct mail is geared to making the sale or closing the deal.

303. If your type of business traditionally eschews using direct mail, you may get a great result from using this unexpected sales method.

304. Increase the response to your solicitation by enclosing something unexpected—like a real dollar bill. This gimmick is still unusual enough to attract attention.

305. Recently, a trade association for the hospitality industry surveyed its members about the effectiveness of the direct mailings they sent to their customers; about 1,100 business owners were surveyed. 90 percent of the respondents mailed just a brochure to their list, and 72 percent of these businesses claimed that the mailing was a success. Sixty-seven of these businesses reported that mailing a brochure worked best to convert new customers. Keep these figures in mind the next time that you plan a direct mailing.

306. Whenever you send a brochure or other sales material to a cold contact, try to include a brief handwritten note on a smaller piece of paper from a notepad. This will help your brochure get past the secretary screeners.

307. If you want wedding business, canvass the engagement notices in the newspaper every week. Send a personalized letter offering reduced rates for your products or services along with a special package for the bride and groom. You might even want to set up a bridal registry service, something that even businesses like electronics shops might offer. If you get their business, send them a free gift on their first anniversary.

308. Send an anniversary card to all your new customers on the occasion of the first time they did business with you. This will involve a fair amount of record keeping, but your customers will be amazed that you remembered them. To increase their amazement, include a special offer or a discount coupon.

309. Whenever a prospective customer turns you down, send him a letter anyway that thanks him for his time. You will be remembered for this.

Direct Marketing on a Budget

310. Test new ideas on a small audience before you spring for a larger one. For instance, mail to 500 people, not 5,000. If the mailing pulls, then mail to the rest with the same offer, or fine-tune your presentation.

311. Postcard mailings—to announce sales, invite customers to a special event, or whatever—are an effective and relatively inexpensive direct mail medium. Use both sides: attention-getting graphics on one side, your message on the other. Offer a prize or discount for customers who bring in the postcard (this is how you can judge the effectiveness of the campaign).

312. If you only do a limited number of direct mail promotions each week and don't want to stock up on pre-printed envelopes with a specific teaser, consider purchasing stickers or a preinked rubber stamp with as many variations as you want.

313. According to some experienced marketers, a good response rate for direct mail is 1 percent. Your budget should be geared to this expected level of return; this is why many experts frequently advise that the price of your offer should never fall under $30.

314. Some entrepreneurs think that they have to pay for return postage on their reply envelopes, but this can become expensive for a small business. Generally, people don't object to using their own stamps, although some mail order experts assert that it does cut down on the response rate.

315. If you can't afford to mail more than 100 pieces at one time, use these smaller mailings as an excuse to personalize each letter.

316. Small businesses that are trying postcards are getting great results. As one entrepreneur said, "Who *doesn't* read a postcard?" Mail first to your house list; then rent or trade a mailing list if you want to increase your results. Make your postcards as personalized as possible: write out a set number yourself every day, or get a typed or written message printed on them at a print shop, or print up labels and slap them on the cards when you're on the phone.

Cooperative Direct Marketing

317. If you produce a catalog, you can increase your exposure and cut costs by involving a complementary business in the fray. For example, one company convinced a clothing manufacturer to provide them with clothes for their catalog shoot. The clothing manufacturer got a credit line and increased exposure in the catalog. The clothing firm also paid for some of the production expenses and received a certain number of catalogs to use to promote their company. Both companies benefited.

318. Card decks—a collection of postcards that are a cooperative version of direct mail, where a number of different businesses make their offers that are packaged together in one mailing—have grown from relative obscurity five years ago to a popular form of direct mail that addresses both consumers and businesses. If you've decided to advertise in a card deck, test two different offers in the same mailing, with one offer going to half of the addressees and the other to the remainder.

319. If you're advertising your business in a card pack, it may be worth the extra placement fee to get your card inserted near the top of the pack.

320. It's important to put a photograph of your product on your card, especially if your company is not widely known.

321. Some small-business people are creating their own card decks by teaming up with other entrepreneurs in their area or in their fields. To create your own card deck, canvass businesses whose products would complement yours in a bulk mailing, and then combine all the businesses' house lists. Divide the costs equally, and depending upon the size of the list, you should be spending a lot less than a card deck producer would charge.

322. The next time you do a direct mailing, offer a business colleague with a complementary product or service the opportunity to include a brochure or letter about her business in your next mailing. Don't charge her anything for it but instead say that you'll accept a fee equal to 10 to 15 percent of their total sales as payment. Many businesspeople will like this because it means no money up front, while you'll like it because you get paid for sending out a mailing to your own customers.

323. When considering joining forces with another company on a direct mailing, make sure that your products and/or services are complementary and not competitive.

Using Direct Mail Incentives

324. Always offer a free gift with the purchase of a direct mail offer. These days freebies are so ubiquitous that people almost expect them.

325. If you use a direct mail piece to get people into your store, include a special coupon for a free item that they can redeem only upon presentation of the coupon in person.

326. If you sell by direct mail, offer customers who order items as gifts the option of free gift wrapping.

327. To entice your prospective customers not to throw out your direct mail piece immediately, include a small item that they will want to keep around. This could be a bookmark or a tip sheet designed to help the reader do something better. The free gifts come later when they place the order, but it's important that you entice the reader not to throw out your direct mail piece just yet.

328. Whenever you fulfill an order, make sure to include another catalog and/or a special sales sheet that includes limited-time offers (two to four weeks).

329. Your latest mailing piece was sent over a month ago and still you have no tangible results. It's time to get serious: call up a selected number of people on your list and ask them what would make them respond to the deal you offered in your mailing piece. It may be a variation on the theme, a cheaper price, or something more luxurious or more spartan. Be prepared to offer it to them on the spot. At the very least, you should take note of their comments for planning future marketing strategies.

330. Make it easy for people to respond to your offer. Even though most of your orders may come in over your 800 line, it's always a good idea to look at other order forms from the direct mail solicitations that you receive.

Timing Your Mailing

331. Determining how often you're going to mail a promotional piece to your list of regular customers is considered an art in some circles. You have to mail often enough to keep your name visible but not so often as to annoy people for whom one mailing is plenty. Let the rhythm of your business determine how often you will do a mailing. A special sale announcement could be sent every couple of months or as seasonal events dictate. Your business might hold a monthly contest; then, of course, you'll want to mail every month.

332. If you're doing a mailing toward the end of the year, your copy should demonstrate how the reader can improve his personal life or business in the new year using your product or service.

333. For some reason, studies show that direct mail packages that arrive on Tuesday receive the highest response, so time your mailing to see if this is true.

334. Direct mail professionals frequently say that January and September are the best months for a high direct-mail response rate. Of course you could always take the contrarian approach and figure that because there are fewer direct-mail pieces going out in other months, your offer will tend to stand out more.

335. According to many of the big catalog companies, the ideal time for mailing a catalog for holiday buying is the third week of November; your response rate may plummet if you mail outside this narrow time frame.

336. Timing is everything when it comes to mailing your promotional piece to potential customers. Direct mail pros believe that the best months to send out a direct mailing are January and October, while the worst are May and June.

ADVERTISING

～

If you're like most people, you probably think that advertising is the form of marketing to which you should direct most of your marketing time and money.

Not all advertising is the same, however, and it's a good guess that one type of advertising—for instance, radio—might work better for your business than another, like print. This is why if you choose this route for either the majority or a tiny percentage of your marketing budget, you should plan carefully and strategically in order to get the most for your advertising dollar. Here's some help.

The Best Medium for Your Message

337. Don't always choose the most obvious section or program for your advertisements. One successful automobile dealer advertises in the business section of the Sunday paper instead of the automobile pages. His ad stands out because there are no other car dealers advertising in the section.

338. If you're undecided between magazine and newspaper ads, if you don't need immediate results, go with the magazine advertising for its long-term value. Magazines have a habit of sitting around in living rooms and dentists' offices, and many businesses receive orders from magazine ads that are more than two years old.

339. Target your advertising: you don't have to advertise in every magazine that is remotely related to your business, nor could you afford to. Each year, you should try to concentrate on promoting just *one aspect* of your business through your advertising program, and focus on one or two publications that will promote this angle most effectively.

340. Target your audience. It might temporarily inflate your ego to advertise in your area's ritziest, most expensive publication, but if that publication's market is not *your* target market, you're wasting your money. Read the demographic information that comes with each publication's media kit, and match up the demographic profile of your customers with the type of publication that they're likely to be reading.

341. When choosing a radio station or publication to run your ads in, choose unconventional stations and publications. For instance, people who are interested in science fiction also tend to be interested in the latest technological products, whether that means the latest computer or panels for solar energy. In this case, science fiction publications would probably work well, as would placing ads in newsletters that go to science fiction aficionados.

342. When considering radio or TV advertising, you should always opt for thirty-second ads over sixty-second ones. A thirty-second ad requires that you get to the point, while a sixty-second ad will allow you to tell a story. In most cases, however, the longer time slot is not necessary. Besides, the listener's attention span is more attuned to thirty-second ads since radio and TV ads today are thirty seconds long.

343. If the name of your business resembles a cultural icon, target your marketing around this identity. For instance, radio ads for a flag and banner company called Bannerman mimicked the old Superman commercials, complete with echoes and sound effects. People flocked to the store, quoting the ad. One customer even wore a Superman suit to the shop to place his order.

Your Advertising Budget

344. Make your ads perform double duty by turning them into flyers that you can later use as handouts or posters. Just blow the ad up to fit the space; no additional design work is necessary.

345. Sometimes the cheapest advertising vehicles are the most effective. Get in touch with a premium company and purchase a thousand pens or bookmarks that are imprinted with the name of your company as well as your phone number. Then give them to everyone you meet. Pens have a way of disappearing and may end up in the pockets of people who are in a position to make a significant purchase from you.

346. Ask sales reps from competing publications or radio stations to design a media marketing plan for your business, that is, a plan that dictates where you should direct your advertising dollars. Many reps will do this anyway, of course, giving the biggest percentage of the pie to themselves. Whether or not you follow through is up to you, but you'll get lots of suggestions and ideas for free and no time spent.

347. If you place ads frequently in your local market, you may get approached by an advertising agency who will want to help you out. If the ads that you have been writing and designing have worked well, it's wise to continue on this path. Unless you're planning to expand nationally, chances are that you won't have the budget for an agency to take you seriously anyway.

348. You can barter advertising time or space: a balloon business works with one of the local radio stations to help promote its remote radio broadcasts by providing balloons to hand out. They both keep a tab. When it's built up, the balloon company schedules some radio advertising.

349. If you have the budget for a relatively large ad, but want more oomph, consider breaking up the space into three or four ads and inserting them throughout the same issue of the paper.

350. Contrary to popular belief and to what ad sales reps say, if an ad doesn't pull for you after a couple of appearances, your response rate surely isn't going to improve after the seventh insertion. So give it a shot if you think it might work, but pull the ad before you start to lose a significant amount of money.

351. If you're planning a classified ad, test it by running the ad on different days of the week to see if one day brings better results than others.

352. Try not to go overboard with abbreviations in a classified ad unless you are sure they are universally understood by readers.

353. Before you decide to place an ad in a particular publication, get a back issue from six months and a year before the current issue. Compare how many ads are still running.

354. In most cases, advertising is used to increase consumer awareness in the long run, and not for an immediate spike in sales. Repeat this mantra to yourself each time before you sign a contract to place some advertising; if you spring for an ad in a more expensive publication and think you'll generate enough sales to pay for the ad, think again. So be sure of your intentions before you confirm an advertising placement order.

355. It is possible to save up to 75 percent on advertising. You can negotiate for better ad rates off the rate card, especially if the issue's closing date is near and there's still empty space to fill. Ask for special rates for new advertisers, frequency discounts, and cheaper special sections. You can also ask to delay your payment until the issue goes to press. Most people simply don't ask and end up paying full price.

356. Per-order advertising may be the best way to go for a small business on a budget. With this method, you pay the magazine or TV station a percentage of your sales instead of a flat-rate advertising fee; orders usually go to the publication or station directly, and they take their cut and send the remainder on to you. One big advantage in arranging a per-order ad with a TV station or publication is that you can use this as leverage with your other distributors and wholesalers by letting them know that your products are advertised in these other media.

357. If you can swing it, spread your ad over several continuous pages—full page if you want to get extremely extravagant—in one issue. These multipage ads are sure to gain attention.

358. Never agree to anything that's marketing related over the phone. Many businesspeople report that salespeople will call them up several times a month to solicit advertising; but no matter how tempting it sounds, if it's that important, have them meet you at your office on your turf. This way, you won't spend money on marketing programs that you don't thoroughly investigate first.

359. Whenever you take your first glance at a publication rate card, take a deep breath and when you talk to the sales rep, tell her that you'll pay half of the rate for the space that you want. She may laugh, but at least it provides you with a starting point.

360. Whenever you're unhappy with the results that a particular ad has brought, let your ad sales rep know. In an effort to make you happy, the publication may just run your ad again for free in order to keep you as a customer.

361. To ensure that you're not throwing your advertising dollars away, be sure to schedule your ads on the days when you are open for business. People will rarely call or stop by the next day if you're closed on the first one.

362. Advertising can be the most expensive way to reach customers, so think of it as a spice, not the main course of your marketing program. After all, most businesses advertise, but the vast majority do not take the time that's necessary to make their marketing—and therefore their businesses—stand out.

Writing and Designing Your Ad

363. Anything that promises the customer that she can have something fast is bound to increase the response to your ad. But don't just say "fast," be specific: "Ten minutes a day," or "Three quick sessions each week," will do more to build up your customer base than almost anything, if they're interested in your product.

364. Can you mention the word *free* in the headline of your ad? Whenever possible, do so, because this word tends to bring in more customers than any other.

365. Clarity in advertising sells products while vagueness only confuses people. Before you send the final proof of an ad off to a magazine or newspaper, show it to ten different people. If any of them expresses the least bit of confusion, then your ad is not clear enough.

366. If one of your competitors goes out of business, advertise your business as an alternative and offer a special discount as an incentive to your competitor's old customers.

367. One well-kept secret in print advertising is that the smallest typeface that you use in your ad should always be bigger than the typeface used most often by the paper.

368. An effective ad inspires potential customers to take action now, preferably with a phone call to your 800 number.

369. Whenever you set out to write ad copy, don't just tell what you're about, tell the potential customer how using your business will improve his life in some way.

370. Sometimes, annoying advertising works best. Remember Mr. Whipple and "Please don't squeeze the Charmin"? A local pizza restaurant has one radio commercial in its repertoire, and it's more than ten years old. Local college students wrote the song, recorded it on equipment that had seen better days, and only occasionally managed to hit the right note. It is a truly obnoxious commercial. Yet, it's been running for years; it must be effective.

371. Make your offer at least three times in the ad. Many ads fail to present their offer clearly, which is a certain waste of money.

372. If you own a service business where you're in the businesses of solving your customers' problems, the most effective form of advertising is to use a case history to show exactly how you did it. The more specific you are—i.e., stating how you saved your client this much money or that much time—the better your ads should pull.

373. In all your advertising, offer a 100 percent money-back guarantee and back it up with quality to match. Few, if any, people will take advantage of your offer over the course of a year.

374. When writing your advertising copy, always remember the simpler and shorter, the better. The size or length of an ad will usually limit you, but make sure that your audience knows exactly what it is you are saying in your ad.

375. The headline or first sentence of your ad will be particularly effective if it takes the form of a question that your potential customers may be asking. For example, "Where Can You Find a Better Mousetrap?" Your ad holds the answer.

376. If your headline doesn't ask a question, then make it the enticing first line of a story that continues in the body of the ad.

377. First-person testimonial-style headlines also work well to attract a reader's attention.

378. Make your ads stand out through the use of a series, especially if the content of the ad focuses on the whimsical and not the hard sell. For instance, there's a hardware store in my area that places a display ad in the local weekly classified paper. Most of the ad space consists of a four-stanza poem, usually about the recent weather or upcoming holidays. In fact, the only mention of the business is its name, the address, the phone number, and the hours of operation. They run it every week, so it must work.

379. Win loyal customers by advertising what you *don't* have. For instance, an inn in Vermont includes this note in its ad: "We do not have TV, phones, kids, traffic, or noise."

380. One successful design element for a print ad is to place it in a frame or distinctive border. Don't make it seem as though your ad is just floating; put it in a box.

381. Another way to make your ad stand out is to shade the background in gray or a light color.

382. Many art directors today use reverse type in their ads, where the background is dark and the letters are light.

383. Sometimes, the availability of free and/or convenient parking is the one factor that will make or break a customer's decision to visit you. If this is an important issue where you live, play up in all your advertising sales literature the fact that there's plenty of parking around your business.

384. Studies show that about half of us make a purchase decision based on pure emotion while the other half tend to operate in a more logical fashion. Is it possible to make your ads and other promotional material appeal to both approaches? If not, then you should seriously consider writing and designing two different ads to appeal to these groups.

385. Look at the section of the publication you want to advertise in; when designing your ad, do something that is the complete opposite of what your competitors are doing. For instance, if the other advertisers are just describing their businesses without making a special offer, then your ad should stress a discounted offer with a deadline in order to make people respond and to make your ad stand out.

386. When designing an ad, make sure that the body of the ad is serif type—that is, each letter has a little flag on it—while the headline should be in sans serif type. This is standard ad design, and straying from it may cause readers to decide that it's too difficult to read.

387. Make sure that you use upper- and lower-case letters whenever possible. Headlines and body text in all caps are frequently difficult to read.

388. Whenever you need an ad written and/or designed for a newspaper or magazine, the ad sales rep might suggest that you save a few bucks by having one of the publication's staff designers do the work for you. You're better off designing it yourself, or having someone else do it for you. Most staff artists will not give your ad the special attention you require, and since the designer is used to working in quantity, the lack of time spent on your ad will usually be obvious.

389. Make your classified ads stand out with a knockout headline. Two places that come to mind are the back pages of the Boston *Phoenix* and New York's *Village Voice*, which are nothing *but* classified ads. Offer a special package or killer price, and make it ridiculously easy for readers to buy from you, especially if you're outside their area.

390. Often, a photograph of you or the item you are selling will enhance the credibility of what you're trying to say in your ad.

391. If you don't want to use a photo of yourself in your ad, try to run a photo of happy, smiling people who are enjoying themselves at your business.

392. If you can tie in a current event with the topic of your ad, you will gain attention. Better yet, change your ad each week to reflect the top stories of the last seven days.

393. Just like those popular diet books and programs that claim you'll lose ten pounds in ten days, your ad should deliver a promise to the customer. What can your product or service do to improve the buyer's quality of life? This is what every ad should address.

Print Advertising

394. Call up your newspaper to get a calendar of upcoming special sections. Frequently these are either seasonal calendar tabloids, bridal inserts, or flyers on new cars. People reading these circulars are actively interested in the subject, so you'll have a greater response from your ad.

395. Try to have your newspaper ad appear as close to the horoscope column as possible. Many people report that they turn to this feature of the paper first. It may cost a little extra for this specific placement, but many businesses that try this technique discover that the additional price is well worth it.

396. When advertising in the White Pages, make your ads stand out by adding an extra informational line to your listing and/or setting the whole thing in boldface. Bold and all capital letters are best.

397. Run a series of teaser ads that tell a story, and then insert them all in the same issue of the paper. It can be one long sentence broken up to fill three or four display ads, but you should make it enticing so that if people catch one ad where the text has ellipses around it, they'll have to flip back and ahead in the paper to catch the entire ad.

398. Create an effective series of ads that reads like a novel. A bookstore owner in Lebanon, New Hampshire, takes out a half-page ad each week in the local shopper, and each week she tells how one fictional family uses some of the books in her shop to take advantage of the seasons.

399. Before you look into taking an ad out in a national publication, test it first by running the ad in one or more of the publication's regional editions. If the ad pulls well, then you can feel safe investing in several more of the publication's regional editions, or even springing for the national edition.

400. Before you spend money in the Yellow Pages, check through the category where you plan to run your biggest ad. How can you make your own ad similar but just a bit fancier? Can you make it just a little bit bigger than the others? Or add a logo that will catch the eye?

401. Bulleted lists of benefits make the most effective print ads. Combined with a time-limited discount offer, the ads can be almost foolproof in conveying your message to your audience.

402. Ads in the Yellow Pages can be very formulaic due to restrictions by the publishers. It's important to stand out from other ads with strong design elements and intriguing headlines.

403. In the Yellow Pages, borders are extremely important so that a reader's eye will be attracted to your ad. So make the borders thick and the margins between the copy and border as wide as possible to draw the reader to your ad and away from other ads that aren't as bold.

404. Change your Yellow Pages ad every year in some way to show readers that you keep up-to-date.

405. Can you make your ad resemble an article? Even though the magazine will require you to place the word *advertisement* at the top of such an ad, laying your ad out in columns and including lots of text will encourage people to read it.

406. Coupons are proven to temporarily increase sales. They are also an effective form of advertising to people who have never clipped a coupon in their lives. A recent study conducted by Robert Leon of Ohio State University showed that sales of a company's product increased overall, whether consumers used a coupon to purchase the product or not.

407. If you use coupons in your advertising, try to run a different offer with each one in a variety of markets so you can test which ones pull best.

408. Running a lot of little ads is more effective than running a larger ad once. If, however, you're still committed to a large-size ad, schedule it for Sundays when there are more people reading the paper. Then run your smaller ads throughout the rest of the week.

409. Go crazy with headings in the Yellow Pages. If you advertise your business under a wide variety of categories, you'll make it easy for customers to find you. For instance, if your business offers office support to other businesses, you might want to advertise under typing services, secretarial services, computer services, temporary help services, among others.

410. A realtor placed an ad that shows a picture of a man, with his back to the reader, sitting on a snowblower in the act. The text of the ad: "This Ariens two-stage blower cleared the driveway quickly. The paving absorbed the sun's rays and quickly melted the rest. If the wind wasn't right, the house got plastered. You'll see what that looks like in next week's paper, along with the reminder that the house, er, this beautiful English Tudor, is still for sale." Even though the ad didn't show the house for sale, it intrigues readers, some of whom are going to be curious enough to call the realtor to see the house. Certain car advertisements follow the same pattern, showing an enticing environment without ever displaying the item that is for sale.

411. If you advertise in the Yellow Pages, you can also spring for one of the coupons that appear in the tear-out section of most phone books. This will make it easy for you to track the success of your Yellow Pages ad. (Be sure to direct people who read your ad in the main section back to the coupon section.)

412. Coupon advertising helps you gauge response when coupled with a newspaper or magazine ad. Not only will this make it easier for you to track how your ad pulls, it should also increase the number of people who respond to your ad.

413. Where a publication allows, advertise in a complementary section of the newspaper or magazine. For instance, a résumé and job counseling service would place an ad in the help-wanted section.

414. Your display ad will get more attention in a "classified-only" newspaper where it has less competition than in a daily or weekly newspaper.

415. The best position for your newspaper ad is on the right-hand page and above the fold. The worst spot? On the left-hand page below the fold.

416. If you have to choose between an ad that's one column wide and six inches high, and one that is three columns wide and two inches high, pick the wider ad. Long, skinny ads appear more difficult to read while the wider ads appear to take up more space and therefore offer more information to the reader.

417. Place an ad in the local television listings near a show that is related to your business. For example, if you run a kitchenware shop, advertise near the cooking shows and house and garden cable channels.

418. If you know you're going to be quoted or mentioned in an upcoming article, purchase an ad in the same issue in which the story will appear. Be sure to include the contact information about your business that will not likely be included in the story.

419. If you receive a direct mail solicitation from a company that says it's the Yellow Pages and comes complete with the Walking Fingers symbol, do some research before you sign up. There's a good chance that the company is one of the Yellow Pages' hybrid directories that produce nationwide directories with little circulation, and not your local phone company. One way to tell is if the solicitation says "This is not a bill." Another sign is if your telephone number is not included anywhere on the bill. If you have any questions about the offer, contact the Yellow Pages sales rep or business office that is listed inside the front pages of your local phone book.

420. If you have a service business, run a small ad in the business service directory of your local newspaper.

421. Advertise to get business, not to win brownie points with the publication's editorial side. Though the smaller publications may give preferential editorial consideration to advertisers, larger-circulation publications may cite a conflict of interest.

422. If you want to blow half your year's marketing budget on a small display ad in a nationally known magazine, it may actually turn out to be a good investment. Why? You can then blow up the ad and hang it throughout your storefront or send it with brochures and other promotional materials to current and prospective customers.

423. If you're going to spring for an ad in a magazine, try to spend the extra money for a color ad, which can provide your business with a better reputation in some circles.

424. If you're looking to place a display ad in a classified advertising section, look at the ads that are already there and then make yours a half or one inch bigger than the largest ad already there. The reason? In many cases, the largest ad will usually be placed first in the listing, increasing your response rate.

425. If you're on the border between two regions with different telephone directories, try this: Take out a small ad in both of them, track your results, and then take out a larger ad in the directory that pulled better, while omitting your ad in the directory that didn't pull as well.

426. If you're running ads in more than a couple of local newspapers, make a different offer in each, and then run each one for a week before rotating the offer to the next paper on your list. After you complete a cycle, measure which offer pulled best in each publication. Then run them again.

427. If you're thinking of taking out a small display ad in a regional or specialized publication, first check out the types of ads that your competitors are running. If most of them are running one-inch display ads, invest in a longer classified ad, or a bigger display ad if you can afford it.

428. Test different ad styles within the same publication. Change the appearance of your ad from one month to the next to see which one pulls best, or see if you can put two different ads in the same issue with one ad going to half of its readers and the other ad to the other half.

429. Just because there are no businesses like yours advertising in a particular specialty publication doesn't mean you should forgo placing an ad. On the contrary, it may be a great opportunity for you. For instance, a well-drilling company might find great leads by advertising in the real estate section of a newspaper instead of in the business services department of the classified section.

430. Just because you run a business where display advertising is the norm doesn't mean that you need to totally ignore classified advertising. For instance, if you sell books or other information on gardening or unique gardening tools, try a display ad in the appropriate classified section for your products.

431. A newspaper insert may appear to be more expensive than a regular ad, but you can control the markets and areas where it will appear to better target your message. Also, you may be able to make the insert yourself and save money on production.

432. One of the best-read sections in many local newspapers is the "transactions" section which contains boxed display ads from local businesses that are announcing special sales or local nonprofits that are promoting an upcoming show or program. They're large, easy to read, and extremely timely, which is undoubtedly why they are such a well-read part of these papers.

433. Since magazines may sit around on coffee tables and in waiting rooms for years, be sure to put an expiration date on a special sale or promotion. The "limited time" offer will also increase immediate traffic.

434. Track the responses to a mail-order business by coding your address to the publication in which your ad appears. (For instance, an ad in *Country Living* could be either listed in your address as "Department CL" or the "CL" could be combined with your street address or listed as a suite.)

435. The size of your ad in a publication or directory may influence how potential customers regard your business. A recent article told of a customer who chose a company with a smaller ad specifically because she figured that their prices would be lower.

436. Some people feel that classified ads generate inquiries, but do not result in direct sales. But the cost is low enough to reach those customers who respond to classified ads.

437. Try taking out a few ads in some of your very local community newspapers and association and church newsletters. You may be surprised at the sizable response you'll receive.

438. Try this as an experiment: Instead of opting for a display ad in the Yellow Pages one year, expand your listing under each category heading. For instance, instead of just having the name of your business, address, and phone number, add a few lines of descriptive text. People look at the listings under the headings first and then at the display ads, so you may be surprised at how much business you pull in.

439. When deciding where to place your ad in a publication, if you can afford it, choose either the inside front or back covers or the last page of the publication for maximum exposure.

440. Whenever you take out a print ad, always include your fax number, your E-mail address, and your Web page, if you have one.

441. If you're looking for a good wholesaler or distributor, take out an ad in the industry publications for your trade. If the publication has an editorial announcement section, send a press release for inclusion noting any sales successes, PR mentions, etc.

442. Many of the larger catalog companies are now accepting ads from outside companies to place in their catalogs. The cost per 1,000 readers you'll pay is probably higher than what a magazine would charge, but since a catalog is essentially nothing but advertising, you'll be able to expose your business to an audience of proven buyers.

Radio Advertising

443. In radio advertising, if you have the choice between lots of words spoken quickly and few words that are spoken at a more leisurely pace, choose the faster version. It's been proven that listeners tend to pay more attention to an ad if the announcer is speaking faster.

444. Before you approve a radio station's production of your commercial, ask for a tape of it and play it back in your car. Any errors will be magnified, and you can have the station correct them before the ad airs.

445. Try to arrange your ad so that a live announcer reads it instead of having the same taped ad run over and over each day. In fact, it makes sense to make friends with the announcer so that he can deviate from the script, often in your favor.

446. If you hear about a new radio station that's starting in your town, make sure to be among the first advertisers on the station. Initial exposure will be significant, since many people tune in to a new station in its early days to check it out. Also, establishing yourself as an early advertiser will probably go a long way toward gaining you great discounts on advertising down the road.

447. Jingles are surefire ways to imprint the name of your business in the minds of consumers if you plan a long-running radio campaign.

448. When designing your radio ad, strive for copy or lyrics that are onomatopoetic, like the *plop, plop, fizz, fizz* of the infamous Alka-Seltzer commercials.

449. If you're advertising on the radio in a small market, and the radio station creates an ad for you, be careful about using the canned music as background that many stations automatically choose for their advertisers. These music tracks can distract listeners from your message.

450. If you're planning on running a serious ad campaign on the radio, it would be most effective if you could get the radio announcers first to try the product and then talk about it on the air. This is what many of the national diet franchises have done: they provide the radio station with free services for a select few announcers, pay for the ads, and then let the announcers talk about how good their company is.

451. Some people feel that radio ads are more effective when they're run in the afternoon during drive time, as opposed to during the morning commute to work. The theory goes that people are more receptive and relaxed when they've finished their workday. So if your product depends on a receptive audience, you might try both times to see which pulls best.

452. Watch the tone of your radio ads. In small markets, commercials that sound amateurish are almost the rule. In some cases, slick-sounding ads will be a turnoff to locals. In a big city, however, professional and slick is the rule, so if you want to stand out, one way to go is to produce a commercial that deliberately sounds amateurish.

453. When choosing a radio station to run your ad, you may think that there's only one market in your area that's best for you to advertise in, but the truth is that very few people listen to just one station, and most are inveterate station changers, especially in the car. If you are currently running a special that would appeal to one distinct group of people, it's best to choose at least three or four different stations to run your customer campaign on. As always, ask where callers and customers heard about you, and then after this campaign is over, you can redirect your ad dollars to the appropriate station.

454. Whenever you produce a radio ad, never say "Look for our ad in the Yellow Pages under 'carpets,' " for example. Why? There, you'll only be one of many in your field. Better to say "Look for us in the White Pages under '[the first name of your business],' " where it's unlikely that any of your competitors will appear nearby.

Television Advertising

455. When running a TV commercial to promote your business, take a lesson from the cable networks and place your logo and/or the name of your business in the lower right-hand corner of the screen throughout the commercial.

456. If you're advertising on television, make sure that you regularly put the name of your company on the screen several times throughout the spot. Many people mute the sound of the TV during commercials, so this way you'll be able to reach these people.

457. One way to advertise your product on TV at a reduced rate is to place it as a prize on a TV game show.

458. Contact a product placement bureau—there are several in New York and Los Angeles—to place your product on a TV show or movie.

459. If you're developing a commercial for TV and your production budget is limited, go for humor over substance. Not only does humor tend to be cheaper than substance, it also will stick in the viewers' minds a lot longer.

460. On every cable and satellite TV system, there's a channel that runs upcoming program schedules. Some of these accept ads. If they're inexpensive enough, and you can afford a series, test a number of different time slots to see which works best for you. It could be prime time or it could be 3:00 A.M.

461. When you're placing an ad on a TV program, try to place it either during the first commercial break or in the middle of the program. Your worst bets are placing it before the final credits roll or directly afterward.

Outdoor Advertising

462. To increase the number of people who will see your billboard, place it in a spot that is notorious for rush-hour delays.

463. Do you have a product or service that would lend itself to an ad in an airport or bus terminal? If your audience includes businesspeople and executives, this might be one of the most attention-getting ways to go after them.

464. A small ski area in rural New Hampshire has supplied the regional transit company with benches at each of its bus stops. The name of the ski area and contact information is painted onto each bench in the same color and design that the ski area uses on its brochures and other advertising.

465. If your business—like roofing, painting, or renovation—takes place at the client's home or business, offer a discount of 5 to 10 percent if you can place a large sandwich board with the name of your company and phone number on their lawn. Check first, however, with local ordinances that may prevent this kind of advertising, even for a day.

466. Another frequently overlooked way to get the word out about your business is to use those large cardboard panels that are designed to shade the front seat of a car during hot days. Make sure that the name of your business is prominent in addition to some colorful artwork and then hand them out for free to your best customers. And print on both sides of the sign to prevent people from just putting the blank side up in their windshields.

467. If you're advertising on the side of a bus or a bus shelter, make sure it looks good enough to steal. Bus shelter posters that are true works of art are tempting to people who would like to have them in their living rooms. You can get a lot of mileage out of letting the media know that your ads are so good that people are stealing them.

468. If you're going to go for some billboard advertising and your budget permits, go for the special effects: lights, special mechanical devices, cutouts, and art that extends beyond the traditional framework attract more attention than standard billboards.

469. Like billboards and sandwich boards, bumper stickers may seem a little bit too old-fashioned for some, but advertising in this way might mean a wide-open opportunity for your business. Try printing up three different bumper stickers to advertise your business and see which one gets used the most.

470. If you have a sign outside your place of business, make sure that the name of your business is clearly visible from the road. If it is not right out in front of your place of business, be sure to print in huge clear letters exactly how far customers will have to travel to get to your business.

471. Remember the old Burma-Shave signs? To stand out, and to rekindle nostalgic feelings among your customers, try designing a sign patterned after this classic: one word per sign and appropriately spaced so drivers can clearly read each word without slowing down.

472. Billboard advertising should be regarded as a supplement to your other advertising and not as a single, short-term boost to your business.

Cooperative Advertising

473. A local innkeeper and restaurateur gets great advertising absolutely free every week or so. How does he do it? The bank that provided him with the financing to purchase the inn a couple of years ago knew he was happy with the bank's service and so asked the innkeeper and his wife to appear in local ads saying so. The bank is happy, and the innkeeper is happy due to the increase in local exposure.

474. Co-op advertising involves promoting a specific product that your company uses in an advertisement, and receiving financial and other assistance from the manufacturer for the advertisement. In many cases, it affords a small-business owner a way to extend the amount of advertising by sharing some of the space with the national or regional company. From there, the sky's the limit when it comes to figuring out deals. Look at what your business offers its customers and look for a partner who can help you reach them.

475. If you decide to sign up for one of those coupon packs that are sent to consumers through the mail, be sure that you are the only business in your field in that particular mailer.

476. If you accept credit cards, try to get a credit card company to enclose a statement stuffer about your business when it sends out its next cycle of bills. Look through your own bills for examples of promotions that work.

477. Arrange with your local supermarket to place your promotional inserts into each grocery bag (assuming they do the packing). This won't be cheap, but if you're looking for local visibility, this is a great way to blitz your way into the minds of your neighbors.

Other Forms of Advertising

478. Promote special sales or events with signs in your personal or business vehicle's window.

479. Buy an ad in the annual high school yearbook. Though it's best if you can congratulate a specific graduate, placing an ad in the yearbook can bring you valuable community exposure.

480. Premium advertising is more than just mugs and T-shirts. Check out the magazines that specialize in the premium field, like *Business and Incentive Strategies*, to get more tips on how best to use premiums in your own business. This will also alert you to upcoming new advertising specialties that are on the horizon.

481. Don't forget about using baseball caps as an inexpensive and wide-ranging way to promote your business, especially if you have an eye-catching logo or one that is instantly recognizable.

482. Flags have caught on big in recent years, mostly among consumers who hang them out to celebrate a holiday or season, but businesses can take advantage of the visibility and fun element of flags as well. Change them often for best results. You can even get them custom-made so that the name of your business is incorporated into the flag design.

483. For a special Father's Day promotion, a clothing store in Pennsylvania runs advertisements in which they offer customers 15 percent off their purchases if they bring in an old tie. The company then donates the ties to a local job search operation so that young people just starting out get a boost with their wardrobes.

. Give away scratch pads with the name of your business and contact information on them to both current and potential customers. This is a form of advertising that customers will find useful, and it's a great way to get and keep your name in front of them.

485. If you accept credit cards, include this service in your ad.

486. Family restaurants or coffee shops often use place mats filled with ads from local businesses. If you choose this route, make your ad in the form of a coupon so you can track the results.

487. If you subscribe to a magazine, then you've probably received a postcard deck in the mail, which is a collection of ads for different companies, except that the ads appear on postcards that you can fill out with your name and address and then send back to the company for more information. If you're thinking about advertising in a postcard deck, get a sample deck from the company that produces them and then call some of the companies that have advertised in them to find out if they were an effective form of advertising.

488. If you plan to advertise in a postcard deck, make sure that at least one well-known company is also included in the deck. Even the smallest start-up business will benefit by association with large corporations and other credible companies.

489. If your business contains a word that is frequently misspelled, consider taking out an additional listing in the phone book under the misspelled name. The highly successful company Dial a Mattress did just this, simply because so many people were spelling mattress with only one *t*. So whether you dialed 800-MATTRES or 800 MA-TRESS, you were still able to reach the company.

490. Many advertising sales departments offer their advertisers a variety of services, including fax back information for each advertiser, discounts for renting the publication's subscriber list, and advance copies of studies conducted by the publication. These additional services may make an ad very worthwhile.

491. Don't forget to investigate advertising on milk cartons and shopping bags. Incorporate a coupon into the ad to increase its effectiveness.

492. Many consumers won't use bumper stickers and window decals because they're so hard to remove. You can invest in static stickers, which serve the same purpose but can be easily taken off at the end of a promotion.

493. You can be a walking billboard for your own products: wear an item of clothing—a T-shirt, cap, or jacket—with your product name on it wherever you go.

494. To keep track of which of your advertisements pull in the most response, always be sure to ask new prospects where they heard about your company. Classify each ad and article with its own department number and track your responses. Then gear your future advertising and publicity plans toward those markets that pull best.

495. Try offering different prices on a variety of packages to several different markets simultaneously as a test. Frequently, the higher price will bring more business and therefore more profits.

496. Provide your steady customers with a permanent reminder that you exist: a refrigerator magnet, a water bottle, or a key chain. Imprint these with your name, address, phone/fax number, and perhaps your business interest or slogan.

497. Unless you've been asleep for the last twenty years, you've noticed that advertising is everywhere these days, from supermarket shopping carts to movie screens and even the floor of your local supermarket. These may initially appear to be expensive media; however, consider the rate on a per person basis, as you should anyway, and you may find these new types of advertising the cheapest around.

498. Vanity plates for your car are not only fun but they can serve up a potent advertising message twenty-four hours a day. Use abbreviations and both letters and numbers so that you can squeeze the most message out of the space that your state allows.

499. When tracking your responses from advertising, make sure that you allow for seasonal influences and other factors that can skew your results before you decide to run subsequent ads.

500. If you've decided to use premiums and other advertising specialties, like key chains or pencils, to promote your business, your best consultant can be a salesman who works at a premium company. Tell the salesperson about your business and the type of customer you'd like to attract, and then ask her for her ideas based on what has worked for her other customers. He may come up with ideas that you've never thought of before.

501. Instead of just using notepads with your name on them as advertising premiums, use imprinted Post-It notes. They tend to be more interactive than regular scratch pads and also have a high pass-along rate, which will increase your exposure.

502. Whether you're posting flyers on telephone poles or business cards on the bulletin board at the local laundromat, you have to make sure to visit these sites at least once a week to replace missing or defaced pieces. Flyers and cards can get torn down or get covered up within a few hours.

IN-HOUSE PROMOTIONS

Many small-business people like in-house promotions, which are displays and special deals that are offered to customers who enter your place of business, because it is a case of selling to the already converted. Shopkeepers like in-house promotions because they frequently help to increase the amount of a sale to a person who is probably there to make a purchase anyway. An in-house promotion, which can be anything from a special of the day on a blackboard by the cash register or a discount on a second item that the customer purchases, can put ideas into buyers' heads, and the good news is that they tend to be inexpensive and creative marketing techniques.

Product-oriented businesses aren't limited to in-house promotions; service businesses can promote special deals to their customers, too, by offering a sale on a companion product. For instance, a dog groomer could sell a product designed to keep dogs looking good between appointments for 50 percent off with the purchase of a standard grooming session.

Sales and Promotions

503. Be careful that you don't get too carried away with price markdowns. As the fashion industry has recently learned, the danger with discount programs is that people may get spoiled and expect sale prices from you all the time. While there are always people who will only make a purchase when it's clear that they think that they are getting a bargain, many customers don't follow this mind-set since quality and convenience are more important to them.

504. Don't segregate your sale racks from your regular-priced racks, since most customers will make a beeline for the sale racks. Instead, mix them all together, and offer customers a discount on regularly priced merchandise as a reward for their hunting skills.

505. Except in grocery stores, the backs of cash register receipts are an overlooked marketing opportunity. This is an inexpensive place to advertise special offers and promotions, or you can trade space with a noncompetitive, complementary local business.

506. If you have eagle-eyed retail salespeople staffing your floor, try this promotion: Ask them to watch out for customers who regularly visit the store but who haven't made a recent purchase. The salesperson should approach the customer, comment that he knows that the customer hasn't made a purchase lately, and tell the customer about something special that just came in that day. This attention to detail will impress customers, spur them on to buy, and bring them back.

507. Offer the customer a chance to get a 20 percent discount on a purchase made today if she spends a couple of minutes filling out a survey for you.

508. During your slow times, hold a special sale. The director at a spa in Vermont decided to offer half price off its weekly rates for the entire month of June, which is traditionally a slow time anyway. He wrote to the Sales and Bargains Department of *New York* magazine with his offer, and he was written up. He didn't make any money on the deal, but he filled his rooms and actually had a waiting list of people who then might be more inclined to book space during the regularly priced months. And from then on, in all of his marketing, he could say "as featured in *New York* magazine."

509. If you plan to attend a trade show, arrange in advance for your staff to hold a "While the Boss's Away Sale" in your absence.

510. If you offer gift certificates to your customers, make sure they know about it. Print up several signs to promote the fact that you sell gift certificates and then hang them around the store or include them in mailings to your regular customers. You might even want to offer a discount to customers who purchase gift certificates within the first month that you offer them.

511. If you run a store and have a number of competitors in town, and it's their policy not to give out prices over the phone, one of the best moves you can make is to be the only store in town that does give prices over the phone. Just make sure that they're reasonable or at least at or below what your competition is charging.

512. In some bookstores, managers will often place slow-selling titles face out instead of spine out on the shelves so that customers can see them. You can do the same thing, whether it's placing one of your more slowly moving items in a bin on the end of an aisle or offering a particular service in quantity to an existing customer base.

513. Whenever you receive a special item that you're putting on sale, make sure that you have plenty on hand to create a large display that will attract the attention of customers. Strange, but people will hesitate to make a purchase from a small display, whereas a large display sends out positive signals.

Special Events and Services

514. If appropriate for your retail business, have well-respected reference books available for your customers to use; e.g., a medical reference text for a health product store or a collectibles price guide for an antique shop.

515. Take a lesson from the mega-bookstores that have set up in-store cafés, attracting many customers who might just be looking for a place to rest. You don't have to set up an entire café, just a thermos of cider and a plate of cookies will be enough to keep customers relaxed and in a buying mood. Yours doesn't have to be extensive, of course, but offering something out of the ordinary is a nice touch.

516. If you have an in-store public-address system that you primarily use to play music, start looking at it as a marketing tool as well. One of the most effective ways to do this is to hold hourly blue-plate specials throughout your store on busy shopping days. Announce the product, the sale price, and where it can be found. You may get some people staying in the store just so they won't miss the next hourly special.

517. Treat every person who walks through your door as if he or she is already a paying customer. There's many a retailer who's lost a sale by ignoring the needs of people who are "just looking."

518. Try to celebrate at least one holiday each month, even if it's an obscure one. It can encompass everything from Random Acts of Kindness Week (the second week in February) to National Fishing Week (the first week of June).

519. If you're planning a sweepstakes or contest, one way to get some great prizes is to work cooperatively with some other local businesses to provide you with prizes at reduced rates or free for promotional consideration.

520. In-store demos and lessons are a great way to increase sales for a particular item. Almost any product lends itself to this kind of sales technique, but anything having to do with food or cooking related seems to work best. Be creative; it will attract a lot of attention if you conduct a demonstration for an item that people have never seen demonstrated in a store before.

521. Make shopping less of a chore and more a form of entertainment for your customers. A Phoenix-based store called Virtues sells natural skin and body creams and other pampering products, but they also offer services including facials and massages.

522. One good old-fashioned event to generate lots of customer response is to guess the number of jelly beans or whatever in a jar. Position one full month of promotion around this contest, and make sure that everybody who enters the contest receives a coupon for a special offer that is good the month after the contest has ended.

523. One of the biggest turnoffs for many customers is to walk into a retail store and have a salesperson immediately pounce. Of course, indifferent service is not the goal here; however, salespeople can make their presence known without constant hovering. Discuss with your staff the best ways to approach the majority of customers who come into the store and then test a few of them out.

524. If you sell handmade items—crafts, food, artwork, etc.—consider having a regular open house to introduce customers to the artisans and to watch them at work. Knowing the artist frequently makes people more comfortable with buying a painting or other craft.

525. Even if the employees in your store don't wear uniforms, you should at least provide pins or name tags to distinguish them quickly for potential customers.

526. Whenever a customer asks where she can find a particular item, don't just tell her the aisle number or point to it. Personally escort her there and then see if she needs any more detailed information about the product.

527. Whenever a customer is at the cash register making his final purchase, be sure to ask if there is anything else he wanted to buy that day. Frequently, a customer will come into the store but not make all of his intended purchases because he simply couldn't find one or more of the items. Asking at the register can serve as a gentle reminder without the hard sell.

528. Greeting every customer who comes to the door with a simple "hello" and a pleasant "good-bye" when they leave can make a lot of difference in terms of how the customer feels about you and your store.

529. One month out of the year, hold a contest to invite the members of the community to design your window display for you. It will draw more people into the store.

530. Tell your staff to always smile and say "please" and "thank you." Unfortunately, in many areas today, surly service and uncaring employees seem to be the norm and not the exception.

531. Write a letter to those on your house list telling them about the special products and services you've recently provided for a few customers. Go into as much detail as possible. Make them want to call you before they even finish reading the letter. For example, a gourmet food store could tell about the mouthwatering new chocolates they've just imported from Germany, and then describe a variety of ways that other customers have enjoyed them. If you will only be offering the product or service for a limited time, so much the better.

Cooperative Marketing

532. In a retail business, you can barter window display space with another noncompeting business in your area. You display her products in your window for a week or longer while she does the same for you. You will enhance your own display while ensuring referrals from the cooperating business. Some good mixes include a dress shop and jewelry store, or a gourmet food shop with an appliance store.

533. If you know that your suppliers regularly issue coupons for their products, get your hands on as many as you can and scatter them liberally throughout the store. Always have a variety on hand and alert your customers to upcoming coupon specials.

534. If your shop is located in a busy downtown area where parking is at a premium, try to arrange a deal with a nearby garage or lot so you can offer free or reduced-rate parking.

535. If striking graphics are a part of your business, arrange to display framed examples of your work at a local restaurant or other establishment. Place a couple of cards around the room to let people know how you can be contacted.

536. Major manufacturers and corporations pour millions of dollars into in-store promotions—posters, special premium giveaways, and informational cards—that often go unused because the store managers are too busy to keep on top of them. If you're not using them, you're missing out. If necessary, assign a staff member the responsibility of keeping these promotional items visible, placed in different areas around the store each week and rotated regularly to feature seasonal merchandise and special offers.

537. If you need a particular item in order to showcase your existing product, and you find it doesn't exist, then you should invent it. One woman with an aromatherapy business couldn't find an appropriate clay vessel in which to heat the oils, so she commissioned a potter to design and make one for her. Offering her customers this unique package helped increase her sales overall.

538. Always be thinking about cooperative ventures with other businesses in your area. For instance, an auto parts store that carries a great line of wax and cleaning products may be able to rent a small space in a new-car showroom in order to exhibit the products and display an attractive sign listing the name of the store along with distributing business cards and brochures. Also be on the lookout for unusual cooperative ventures. In some cases, the more unlikely the fit, the more successful you'll be.

Designing Your Store

539. Just because you may be running a retail store that specializes in serious products doesn't mean you can't have a little bit of fun when it comes to merchandising. Bruce Julian of Milton's Clothing Cupboard in Charlotte, North Carolina, uses imaginative fixtures and displays such as a statue in the shape of Yoda from *Star Wars* to display expensive Italian ties and a bear-shaped stool for the salespeople in the shoe department.

540. If you run a retail store, sometimes it's necessary to spend money to make money, even if that means buying merchandise that you know you'll have a hard time selling. One woman who runs a secondhand clothing store in Vermont says that she sometimes buys articles of clothing that will look wonderful in the store and not because she thinks that they'll sell. It works: the store looks like a fashionable Victorian grandmother's attic, with clothes that are classic and in style. The owner knew all along that she wanted to have an enchanted Alice in Wonderland type of place, and her large repeat business proves her out.

541. Here's an idea for a new way to get attention for the posters you use in your store to promote specials: Hang them at an angle. People will probably ask you about them, which gives you the opportunity to explain specials to them in detail.

542. If your store doesn't already have a sign that you can flip over or turn on that says "Open," run, don't walk, to your nearest hardware store to pick one up. It's also a good idea to post your hours of operation nearby.

543. If your store is located in an urban area where it's necessary to pull steel gates down over the windows each night, take advantage of that unused space by having a local artist paint a mural or sign that depicts your business in some way.

544. Live window displays work wonders, whether it's a pet store that features live puppies and kittens in the window, or a live-action model who spends the day working on a product or service that your store sells.

545. Next to lighting, nothing creates mood in a retail outlet better than music. Depending upon the mood you are aiming for, you can choose big band, classical, blues, country and western, top forty, or even retro music. Think of the image that you want to convey to customers and then choose your music accordingly.

546. Nothing is more overlooked in the world of small businesses than lighting. More than anything else you can do to help market your small retail business, lighting can be the difference between drab and stunning. Proper lighting will create a sense of warmth, cleanliness, and order that is appealing to the eye. Very subtle corner lighting can take sharp edges away. When full of shadows, a room can look cold and less than inviting, which will do nothing to increase your revenues. Most important, people have to be able to see what they're buying, and good lighting is vital.

547. One unique idea that may help increase overall sales for you if you have a shop is to model your store layout after the self-guided nature trails located in many parks. For instance, a clothing store would lay out a floor trail that leads a customer from skirts and blouses and dresses to accessories and finally to the makeup counter. Think up ways in which you can utilize this technique in your own business; clear signage is all that you need.

548. Snazz up a window display by keeping it well lit at night, or keep a TV monitor running a promotional loop even during off-hours. This will help build foot traffic during the day by piquing the curiosity of people who view your promotions at night.

549. What is a movie set without props? The props that you use to decorate your store could be as simple as a candelabra or a set of children's blocks to an entire themed room. Much like music, props will elicit a certain feeling from your customers and create a mood. If properly executed, the mood you create will be a pleasant one. People will want to come back just to recapture the feeling.

550. When designing promotional signs to place around your store, make sure that they are consistent. For instance, for permanent signs, make sure that they always appear in a particular typeface and color with a distinctive border. Weekly and monthly specials, however, should be in another color-coded design with their own distinct typeface and border so that customers are alerted to this special that is a limited-time offer.

551. Whenever your business is mentioned in the media, make sure that your customers are aware of it. You can frame a magazine or newspaper article and display it prominently in your storefront or blow it up to poster size. For a TV appearance, get a frame from the show reproduced or a photo of the host for display.

552. If you have a retail storefront and wish to increase its visibility from the road, there are some things you can do; e.g., install window awnings with your store's name printed on the front or top.

553. One gourmet food store in a touristy area of Maine changed the interior walls of the store from dark green to white to enhance the store's visibility from outside.

554. Make the sign for your business as large and noticeable as you can. You don't want to be obnoxious about it, but you don't want the lettering to be so small that

MARKETING ON THE INTERNET

～

Since 1995, use of the Internet as a business marketing tool has gone through the roof; for small-business people, there's almost no way to ignore it as a way to gain exposure for your business. A lot of attention has been paid to the potential of the Internet as a way to make money. Amidst all of the information, however, one thing is for sure: You can't just toss a Web page up and wait for the orders to pour in. Many potential customers will use your site as a way to perform initial research about your company, and then call your 800 number for a paper catalog and place an order by writing a check and sending it via snail mail. At this stage of the game, the Internet offers novelty and represents yet another way for people to get information.

Many big businesses pour thousands of dollars into the development of their Web pages, and then get most of their satisfaction from the fact that they appear to be a technologically hip company. As a small company, you can't afford to be this complacent. The good news is that by combining traditional marketing methods with some high-tech techniques, your Web page can do more than stand as a bits-and-bytes version of your paper marketing materials.

Before you spend the time and money to establish a presence on the World Wide Web, you should be clear about your intentions. Many businesses have jumped onto the Web either because they sell pots of instant gold or felt they had to do it because everybody else was doing it. So consider your reasons for going on-line and whether it will be worthwhile intrinsically to you, at least in the near future.

Beware of companies that sell advertising space on the Web or other Internet sites and inform you that your ad will be able to reach thirty million people. I don't know of any site that generates that much traffic, and besides, that audience is usually spending a lot less time at any one site than they would with another form of media. You're better off spending the money to develop your own Web site.

Though many businesses are rushing headlong into establishing Web pages, if you're just getting your feet wet in cyberspace, start small with just an E-mail address through one of the on-line services. You can then expand your own presence by advertising in an established electronic shopping mall until you become familiar with some of the nuances and subtleties of using the Internet.

Marketing Yourself Through E-Mail

556. Every time you send a piece of E-mail, whether it's to an individual or to a newsgroup or mailing list, be sure to post a detailed signature that not only describes what you do but also includes all the different ways that you can be contacted. Include your name, the name of your business, and your E-mail address.

557. One way to get flamed, or receive lots of nasty E-mail, is to push your business in an obvious manner. It's better to serve as a resource so that other people will come to you in order to learn more about what your business can do for them. For instance, when you first join a newsgroup or post a message to a forum or Internet bulletin board, don't just tell everybody what it is that you do. Not only will you be flamed but your subsequent motives and participation in the group will be suspect. Instead, find a post with a question that is easy for you to answer and applicable to your field.

558. There are a number of E-mail services—Juno is one—that offer users free unlimited E-mail in exchange for having an ad tacked onto every E-mail message. Contact the providers to see how you can be a part of this as well as get involved in future projects the provider may be planning.

Your Web Site

559. Be sure that you list your site with as many Web search engines as you can, like Lycos or Yahoo (http://www.lycos.com; http://www.yahoo.com). Tens of thousands of Internet users rely on these directories each day to search for Web sites in a particular category, so be sure to list your Web address, also known as a URL, on as many search engines as you can.

560. Do you want to market your company on-line or make sales? If marketing is your goal on the World Wide Web, you should focus on making your pages an attractive and interesting extension of your business. Marketing on the Web is content oriented, so you will have to get users involved and give them something to do. Some popular tactics are newsletters with useful information about your products and services, interactive games, and contests.

561. On your Web site, encourage customers to post notes in a special section devoted to customer feedback. As is the case in other media, testimonials also help increase revenues on the Web.

562. Once you get your Web site up and running, you're going to receive a certain number of hits from people who are browsers. Keep them coming back by constantly changing the content of your site. People will only check back a few times to search for new material before giving up because you offer the same old thing.

563. Offer enough information to intrigue potential customers, but don't give away the store. Try offering excerpts or samples from your business in the form of sound or graphics files, and be sure to provide a variety of ways in which Web surfers can contact you.

564. Get free publicity for your Web page by being included in print articles that cover commerce on the Internet. Your name being associated with other companies who market on the Internet will give you credibility and increase hits to your page from browsers.

565. People who write a letter or call an 800 number to receive more information are used to waiting a week or two to receive a catalog or other sales materials. However, since the basic essence of the Internet is its speed and accessibility, it's even more vital that businesses respond promptly to customer queries.

566. Go to www.submit-it.com to list your URL in more than two hundred search engines within minutes.

567. You'll find that the cost of attracting and keeping a new customer via the Internet is lower than that of other traditional means of marketing, since you don't have to invest in catalogs and other marketing materials or postage. Therefore, you may want to pass some of your savings along to your customers who buy from you solely on-line.

568. Some experts believe that in order to really succeed in increasing your revenues on the Web you should specialize in promoting one product or service per site. They feel that a too-general page and content won't be enticing enough to customers.

569. To entice traffic to your Web page, before you actually try to sell anything, use the page to provide information about your field to potential customers. Add to this content every few days while promoting the page through links, and then make a big deal about the unveiling of your product listings.

570. When it's time to determine the content of your Web page, keep in mind that almost anything goes. Since people prefer to get their information in different ways, you should give it to them by providing graphs, text, surveys, pictures, and maps as well as a long list of resources.

571. Whenever you collect inquiries over the Internet, be sure to make those names part of your marketing mailing list just as you do when customers call in or write for more information. Then, you can send announcements and other news to this electronic mailing list.

Establishing Links and Cooperative Marketing with Other Web Sites

572. If you're looking for a niche publication to market your business, the most specific niches can be found in the on-line publications, also known as zines, on the Internet. For example, you can check out Women's Wire at http://www.women.com for an avid audience of technologically hip women, or Addicted to Noise at http://www.addict.com if you market products related to the music industry.

573. If you have a Web page, establishing a network of links to and from other pages that cover subjects that are similar to yours is welcome and almost mandatory. This will help Web surfers learn about your page. It's important to get links on pages that are particularly important in your field, but don't go overboard. If one of your links sounds more compelling than your own page, the people who visit your page will be tempted to go right to your links.

574. Look into placing your product or service on one of the electronic shopping malls that are available through on-line services such as CompuServe and America Online. In fact, there are many special-interest forums and boards within each on-line service that have their own electronic malls or stores, so it's a good idea to investigate these too.

575. Once you have your Web page up and running, start to think about the other pipelines through which you could promote your business. For instance, FAQs (frequently asked questions) are regularly posted on newsgroups and in other forums. These additional methods will help you reach the largest audience possible.

576. Provide free information to on-line services and Web sites in exchange for a promotional announcement about your business. For instance, the editor of a newsletter on rural life supplies a home-and-garden on-line publication with free excerpts from the newsletter to run on the Web site each month.

577. Spend at least a few hours each week surfing the Web. Follow the links with other sites to see where they go. More often than not, you'll discover a business, association, or a publication that is a natural market for your business.

Marketing Yourself as an Expert On-Line

578. If you can provide advice to people who are interested in your industry, consider hosting a chat on one of the on-line services like America Online or Compuserve. Locate the folder or forum that covers your field and then send an E-mail to the moderator, offering to host a chat on a particular aspect of your field. You won't get paid for it, but it's a great way to gain exposure and to draw prospective business.

579. Responding to queries on the message boards and forums of the on-line services is an easy way to build up presence as an expert and therefore promote your business. Your responses should always be signed with the name of your business, location, and phone number.

580. If you are involved in what others frequently consider to be a glamour business, like running a country inn, one way to market your business is to post your own letter about the reality of your life as a business owner to a newsgroup or bulletin board of aspiring innkeepers, and watch the responses roll in.

581. Join a newsgroup pertinent to your field and become a frequent participant, answering the questions of others by posting directly to the newsgroup within twenty-four hours. You never know who is watching and could turn out to be a valuable customer or reference.

Internet Advertising

582. Banner advertising is a way that Web surfers can find their way to your Web page. Usually, the Webmaster of a page will charge another company for a certain number of hits for an ad on the main screen of a Web page. When users click on your ad, they are instantly transported to your page. Other effective advertising methods will undoubtedly develop, but this method has served as one of the early success stories in Web advertising. As advertising on the Internet continues to redefine itself, one surefire way to receive good exposure is by advertising on a related business's main screen.

583. Before you decide to advertise on another Web page, visit the site for about a week to see if the information changes regularly. If it's not updated frequently, visitors are not likely to return to see your ad.

Market Research On-Line

584. Before pitching an idea to a publication, check their on-line presence and sift through the archives to see how they've approached this subject in the past. Offering a new twist on a subject they've already covered is a great way to get your foot in the door.

585. Go on-line to the bulletin boards, message boards, and newsgroups that concern your industry and do some market research about what people are looking for from your business. Respond personally to each person who writes, consider their suggestions carefully, and then file their E-mail addresses in a database to use to promote your business.

586. Have a question about a new design for your brochure or a new publicity angle? If you have access to an on-line service, post your idea in the appropriate forum and almost immediately you'll start to receive feedback from some of the millions of people who surf the Net. For instance, if you're considering offering a personal buying service at your store, you can ask other retailers who have done it for advice on a forum for retailers.

587. If you'd like to approach a particular publication about your business to promote it, first check if they have an on-line presence and also if they list the E-mail addresses of the editors. Many editors today are more inclined to respond promptly to E-mail, while they let regular mail languish in the in box. If you send a brief note to an editor via E-mail, you may very well get more press for your business as a result.

SPECIAL EVENTS

People love parties and celebrations, and one of the best ways to market your business is to hold a special event where both your present customers and future ones can have fun and learn a little something about your business.

Most special events require a bit of planning, but again, the time and energy you'll spend will be worth it in an increase in business and goodwill in the community.

Holidays and Seasonal Events

588. Almost every business will do a special promotion tied in with Christmas and other major holidays. Help your business to stand out by celebrating a holiday that few other businesses notice: Halloween, April Fools' Day, or you can even make up your own.

589. Producing limited editions of seasonal specialties frequently results in a boost in revenue. Three Dog Bakery, a company that produces all-natural dog biscuits, makes little burritos for dogs called Akita Tacitas for a southwest sampler that the company sells in May for the holiday Cinco de Mayo. In December, the company sells biscuits in the shape of stockings, reindeer, and candy canes.

590. If you produce a range of products, tailor one of them to a specific time of year, preferably the big Christmas buying season. This will help increase your sales and enhance your opportunities of getting valuable PR. Also, catalogs or distributors looking for seasonal products are more likely to pay attention to your product line.

591. Every year on one day in June, the ice cream maker Ben and Jerry's gives away free ice cream cones at every one of its shops. The lines are out the door, and you can be sure that some of the people who are picking up their free cones will be there the next day paying for one. Make your free day an annual event, too, and watch your business grow.

592. Attract attention by celebrating a holiday out of season. Christmas in July always pulls a crowd, but what about Thanksgiving in March to celebrate the fact that winter is over?

593. If a holiday that would best promote your business doesn't exist, then make it up and promote your business. Get a hold of the book *Chase's Annual Events* to get an idea of all the obscure holidays that have been invented solely as promotional devices: there's National Zucchini

Day, in addition to Take a Cat to Work Day, as well as thousands of other equally obscure holidays. Join the fray.

594. If you're tired of the usual holiday sales and promotions, instead offer a chance for people to truly commemorate what the day stands for. Thanksgiving and Christmas are ideal holidays to develop a promotion that gives people a taste of simpler days without fax machines and beepers.

595. If your town is having a special holiday event, make sure that your staff members dress accordingly. For instance, a nearby town holds a Dickens Christmas Weekend every December. One restaurant has its staff dress up in appropriate costumes.

596. On the anniversary of the day when you first opened your doors for business, do something community minded to attract both the media and new customers to celebrate. It could be a free cookout for the town or a paying event with all proceeds going to charity. Or you could donate a day's profits or service to the needy.

597. Plan an open-house weekend at your business to celebrate an anniversary or some other benchmark. Pull the crowds in with a promotion like the dog kennel that hosted a doggie psychic.

598. Each year, Ocean City, Maryland, hires a team of professional sand sculptors to construct intricate, detailed, expansive sand castles on the beach. People come out of curiosity and spend money in the shops, restaurants, and lodging.

599. To promote your business, you can even create your own special theme week or day to call attention to it. For instance, National Artichoke Day, National Spay and Neuter Day, and thousands of others have been created by special interest groups.

600. Peter Baylies, the publisher of a newsletter for fathers who stay at home to take care of their kids, plans special Father's Day promotions each year. This promotion has also attracted women who have subscribed to the newsletter for the husbands, hoping that they might take the hint and decide to stay at home with the kids.

Seminars and Workshops

601. Book a hall or meeting room to promote a free-admission event that spotlights your business while also providing valuable information to the people who attend. For instance, if you own a kitchen or appliance store, invite a local cookbook author to teach a cooking class. Market the event to local newspapers, magazines, and radio stations and with flyers and posters. Send postcards about the event to all the people on your mailing list, promising a free gift if they attend. Invite them to bring a friend.

602. Can you tie in your product or service with an event that is ongoing at a more established business? A tea expert teamed up with the Ritz Carlton in San Francisco to conduct a regular series of talks about tea at the hotel.

603. If you are organizing seminars or workshops to sell your products or services, you should consider having a strong closer take the podium for the last ten minutes of the presentation. Your talk may have been great, but having another person vouch for you—even if he is an employee of your company—will provide a new perspective on what you've discussed and help increase your sales.

604. Contact an adult community school like the Learning Annex and offer a one-evening workshop about a specialized aspect of your field. Consider this an opportunity to educate potential customers—the students in the workshop—about your business. Offer a discount to students who make a purchase from you within a week.

605. Contact another workshop promoter and offer to present a miniseminar on your area of specialty in exchange for setting up a table in the same room. If you're the only one selling items at the workshop, you may do quite well due to lack of competition.

Community Events

606. If you belong to a trade association, you might consider having an annual open house in order to better educate the public about your industry. One woman in Maine raises llamas and belongs to a statewide llama breeding organization with thirty-five members. Every

June, they hold a "field day" to which the general public is invited. The event draws thousands of people, both curiosity seekers and serious buyers.

607. If you've scheduled a series of talks that are open to the community, send out a press release before the first talk begins. Invite members of the press to attend without charge, if you are charging the public.

608. If you're planning a series of regular talks to the public, issue a press release describing each talk to members of the media as soon as possible after the event. This will help to build traffic for your future events.

609. The businesspeople in one Vermont town created a free-to-the-public dinner concert series. The concerts are held every Friday and Saturday night during the months of February and March, feature storytellers and poets, bluegrass, jazz, and chamber music. The price of admission to the concerts is a donation to the local emergency food bank. Local businesses pledge $25 to $200 to help sponsor the series. Many business owners mentioned that they noticed an increase in afternoon sales from people who were in town to attend the concerts.

610. If your town or community holds a street fair or festival, offer to provide a banner to string across the street for free. The deal is that your name appear on the banner as well, underneath the festival name and dates, and in slightly smaller type.

611. Plan a series of open houses for businesses from your area. These could be either industry-specific or a free-for-all event that you could actually bill as a valuable networking opportunity for all local businesses to gain new business.

612. Sponsor a float in your town's next parade.

613. If you rent a booth at a local one-day flea market or festival, offer a limited-time special connected with the event.

The Details

614. Before you plan your next special event, make sure that it won't bring out the worst in people. A Fort Worth radio station announced that one of the DJs stashed away a number of five- and ten-dollar bills in books located at one of Fort Worth's libraries. A stampede through the stacks ensued, and the radio station later had to announce that it was all a prank. The station had to pay over $10,000 to cover the destruction. No matter what your special event, make sure that you do not alienate local public officials.

615. To promote special events, send a series of teasers to customers to pique interest. The first one could say, for example, "Your company has been requested on the evening of June fourth at our business." That's it. Go from there to spread the information out across a number of mailings. Make the event appear as mysterious as possible, so that people will be compelled to attend just to satisfy their curiosity.

Props

616. Helium-filled balloons imprinted with your company name are a popular marketing tool because they make any occasion an event, and they continue to advertise your name until they're totally deflated.

617. If you're planning a special-event at night, you might want to think about the rental of a searchlight for the duration. With all the high-tech marketing effects that businesses use these days, a searchlight is a bit old-fashioned but it will get you noticed.

618. Today, rental companies have items such as spotlights, complete sound systems, even live animals to enhance your special event.

619. If you really want to attract attention, wear a costume that is appropriate for your presentation or event.

Other Ideas

620. Contests or sweepstakes are a cheap and easy way to collect names for your mailing list in addition to their inherent promotional value.

621. When you exhibit at a flea market, take the products that you would normally classify as seconds to sell there and then discount them at least 50 percent. Some people are attracted to anything that seems like a good bargain, and you'll probably draw customers who wouldn't normally visit if you weren't offering such a great deal.

622. Consider hosting a home party demonstration to sell your product or service, even though it might appear to be an unlikely way to promote your particular business. Make it entertaining, provide refreshments, and be sure to entice the people who attend into buying with free offers, discounts, and incentives for bringing additional customers.

623. If you run a product-oriented business, and a good part of your trade deals with used equipment—like computers or books—you might want to think about sponsoring a swap meet to promote your business and the idea of buying used merchandise.

624. If you run a service-oriented business, don't discount such venues as flea markets and fairs as a way to promote your business. You can bill it as an open-air version of your business to current and new customers. You may be the only one of your competitors attending, which should benefit both you and your customers.

625. A country inn called Adair, in Bethlehem, New Hampshire, sent a postcard that read: "Yet another reason for living in New Hampshire. Residents of New Hampshire deserve a little something extra, like 10 percent off our regular lodging tariff through 1995." Think about how you can turn living in your state into an advantage for your fellow residents.

626. One unique way to promote your business is by staging a picket in front of your place of business. Hire some of your friends or some students to walk around for a couple of hours in front of your store, carrying signs that clearly describe the benefits of your business to passersby. Of course, have someone tip off the media in advance.

627. Run a contest or sweepstakes to increase the visibility of your business. One study has shown that a sweepstakes can actually double the number of bona fide customers over the course of the sweepstakes. First check your state regulations regarding sweepstakes and contests.

628. What kind of special contest can you think of to promote your business? Odor-Eaters conducts an annual smelly sneaker contest and gets an awful lot of media exposure for it year after year. And, Richard Thompson of Thompson's Pet Pasta Products, Inc., a company that sells bagged pasta in flavors that dogs like, ran a national contest: Teach Your Dog to Say "Pasta." Armed with a video camera, Thompson toured the country and invited dogs in thirty cities to make their case. The winner (the dog, the owner, or both!) of the contest gets a two-week trip to Italy.

629. When you sponsor a contest or a sweepstakes, earmark funds not only for a grand prize but also for consolation prizes to everyone who entered. If you're a retail outlet, have the winners come back to your place of business to claim their prize. The great thing is that, when they come back, they're more likely to buy something from you as they pick up their prize, which could be an inexpensive trinket.

630. For whom is your special event? While some may be for current customers, most special events are designed to go after potential customers. And make sure that your event reflects that, from the attractions and decorations all the way down to the food and drink.

TRADE SHOWS

～

Trade shows and expos are a great way to get your business before the eyes of a large number of people who are at the show specifically to buy . . . or to help them decide what to buy in the future. Though getting ready to exhibit at a show requires a lot of time spent planning, and money, on a per-prospect basis, a trade show is one of the best ways to meet with potential clients, as well as touch base with existing customers.

Preparation and Planning

631. If you're thinking about exhibiting at a trade show, visit as an attendee first to get an idea of the other exhibitors and of how well you could do with a booth. Ask the other exhibitors if they come back to the show year after year—a good sign—and check out the booth layout to see where you'd like to have your booth next year.

632. Before you book space in an exhibit at a big trade show, it's a good idea to visit the year before to see the types of displays companies are using. At some trade shows you can get away with a low-tech homemade look, but this approach may work against you at a trade show where the emphasis is on costly, high-tech displays.

633. Before you send in your deposit for a booth at a trade show, call a few of the exhibitors—with businesses both similar and different from yours—from the previous year's show and ask how they did there.

634. Go co-op with another company to save on booth fees and to also gain extra manpower. Some small businesses decide to split the cost of a table or booth with another business that's complementary to their own. Your booth will never go unmanned, for one of you can always be there while the other makes the rounds, and people who wouldn't stop at your booth if you alone were exhibiting may be attracted by your boothmate's business. You'll both enjoy the spillover business.

635. Before the show, contact the show's producer to get a list of the people who have signed up to attend the show. Send them a postcard directing them to your booth and offering them the chance to redeem the postcard for a special show offer.

636. If the show promoter is selling advertising in the directory, then spring for an ad with an enticing headline that causes people to visit your booth out of curiosity.

637. If you can't decide at which show to exhibit, and you have a limited budget for trade shows, ask your customers which trade shows they attend.

638. If your target market lives in a particular region, contact the local convention and visitors bureau there to ask them about upcoming shows appropriate for your business.

639. Consider sponsoring one of the coffee breaks or other events at the show. The promoters will hang a banner with your name or list your name in the show program.

640. Advertising in the show's program is a great way to expand your exposure to the industry before, during, and after the show.

641. If you're planning to rent a booth at a local home show, find out what type of advertising the show promoters are doing. Then arrange to piggyback your own show-themed ads with theirs. For instance, place your newspaper ads that give your booth number on the same page as the ad for the show, if you can.

642. Even if you can't attend a trade show in person, you can arrange to display your product or service in cooperation with another exhibitor. Promise your boothmate a cut of whatever sales result from the show as an incentive to promote your product as his own.

643. One booth exhibitor sent personalized handwritten invitations to 200 of his best potential customers a few weeks before his next show. In each message, he invited each person to stop by the booth and meet him personally. This tactic increased show sales by 300 percent over the previous year, prompting the company to continue with this method in subsequent years.

644. Your promotional material should reflect the product or service you are promoting at the trade show. For example, a car-care product company printed a promotional piece especially for a trade show on chamois cloths.

645. If you have a new display you're planning to unveil at a show, give it a test run before the show to see how long it will take to set up and break down—whether or not union help will be required at the show—and to work out any kinks.

646. Take out a small display ad in the show's program guide. And don't forget to include your booth number, in addition to some information on your location—whether your booth is located at the back of the hallway or near the seminar hall, for example.

647. Two weeks before the date of a trade show, send out a mailing to those on your customer list alerting them to the booth number as well as to any special promotional deals you'll be offering customers at the trade show. Highlighting any new products or services in this mailing is also a good idea.

648. When you send a preshow mailing to your customers, go all out and spring for engraved invitations for your best customers.

649. If you're signing up to exhibit at a show at the last minute, bargain with the promoter to get a better price on your booth.

650. Send your best customers a schedule of the trade show events—on your stationery—along with a map with the location of your booth circled.

651. See if your reps or suppliers are planning to exhibit at an upcoming show. Offer them a percentage of all orders for your product that are taken at the show.

652. Before you leave for the trade show, make a list of everything that needs to be brought or shipped, and then check it three times. One greeting card company brought everything but the envelopes and had to arrange to have them shipped overnight.

653. If the trade show you're attending has a press room for visiting media, make sure that you have plenty of your brochures and press kits available.

654. Some trade show promoters offer joint displays for brochures or products. This might be a good strategy for first-timers who don't want to take out a full display but may attend the show in person. While it's not the ideal way to get your goods noticed, it gives a focal point for reference to those people you meet.

At the Show

655. Although your facial muscles will hurt at the end of the day, it's important that you always smile at a trade show. According to Allen Konopacki, the president of the Incomm Center for Research and Sales Training in Chicago, a person who is smiling will attract the attention of a potential customer from up to twenty feet away. It also makes people curious to find out why you are smiling.

656. Volunteer to participate in the show programs as a workshop leader or facilitator, talking and answering questions about a specific facet of your industry. Invite people who attend the workshop or seminar to stop by your booth to continue the discussion.

657. Even if you don't exhibit at a trade show, you can learn a lot by simply attending the event and participating in workshops and seminars. From this perspective you'll learn to appreciate your customers' concerns and have an opportunity to check out the competition.

658. If you know that some of your biggest suppliers or buyers will be at the show, arrange to provide them with free tickets to a local sporting event or show while there.

659. Hold a contest to give away one of your products or services with a high perceived value, or an item like a

VCR or mountain bike. Make sure that the attendee steps into the booth to fill out the form, and that one of your reps is in attendance.

660. Ask your suppliers if they have any marketing materials you could use to enhance your display at a trade show. Displaying these items will help lend credibility to your own business.

661. While you're at the show, spend some time talking with other exhibitors, exchanging business cards, and discussing possible cooperative ventures.

662. At any trade show, you have to be proactive to get people interested in your product. Instead of sitting behind a table and waiting for prospects to approach you, ask everyone who walks by a question pertinent to your business—something to get them into your booth. Actively solicit people and invite them to call later with other concerns. Trade shows give you a rare chance to interact face-to-face with your customers and prospects.

663. Keep a bowl of candy at your booth. The few seconds that it takes for a prospect to reach into the bowl can be an opportunity for you to give your pitch.

664. While you're exhibiting at the show, make the rounds of the other exhibitors to suggest cooperative marketing ventures like sharing the cost of a direct mailing or carrying each other's products in your catalogs, if appropriate. Collect their business cards and brochures, and contact them during the first week after the show.

665. Attend all of the show-sponsored parties. Socializing with other exhibitors and show attendees can be a great way to meet people you wouldn't otherwise during the bustle of a show day.

666. At trade shows, have visitors fill out an order blank to win a prize from you at the end of the day. The promotion is even more effective if winners must be present to win because you'll get people coming back to your booth, so make sure the prize is worth the effort.

667. Have a giant fishbowl at your booth into which people can drop their business cards to enter a contest where you give one of your products or services away. You can then add these names to your in-house mailing list.

668. If there's a trade show for your industry scheduled for your area, offer to take a news reporter who's familiar with your business to the show, introducing her to valuable contacts as well as providing a running commentary on the exhibitors and workshop presenters. If you see your role as guide, not promoter, you'll get more and better press in the long run.

669. If you run a product-oriented business and have a force of sales reps selling your product, many times they exhibit at shows, charging a small fee to the companies they represent. If your budget is tight, ask your reps at which shows they plan to exhibit.

670. If your targeted trade show is like most, both attendees and exhibitors will be exhausted at the end of each day. One enterprising exhibitor had fun with this by offering free five-minute massages and footbaths during the last hour of the show on each day. You can bet that this brought a lot of people to his booth.

671. A major trade show provides an ideal opportunity to introduce a new product or service. You can then tie in the new item with your show special and alert the media covering the show to your booth.

672. Hire a model—perhaps dressed in an appropriate costume—to circulate on the floors of the exhibit hall passing out flyers or cards inviting people to your booth.

673. Invite attendees to a special party after the trade show is over in the hotel restaurant or meeting room.

674. Make sure that you have a quiet space somewhere near your booth where a member of your trade show team can sit down with a customer to address personally any specific issues away from the hubbub of the trade floor.

675. One adventure travel outfitter who regularly exhibits at trade shows has plates of cookies featured prominently around the perimeter of her exhibit table. Most people would feel it's rude to grab a cookie and keep going, so this extra minute can give you the time to make an impression.

676. One of the hallmarks of a trade show is the mountains of promotional material that attendees carry away with them. Head in the opposite direction and just hand out a business card but be sure to collect the attendees' business cards. Send out appropriate materials and make follow-up calls within a week after the end of the show.

677. To increase your networking capacity, participate in as many pre- and postshow events with other exhibitors as you can.

678. If you exhibit at a high-volume trade show, hire a couple of freelance sales people to help you out. They need to know the basics about what they're selling, of course, but what they may lack in product knowledge they'll make up in sales skills.

679. Though you should be on your feet as much as possible during a trade show, you might want to invest in high stools that you can place at the back of your booth which will enable you to sit down but still maintain eye-level contact with the people who pass by your booth.

680. To attract attention to your booth, you can hire professional entertainment—e.g., a magician, storyteller, or sketch artist. This is a great way to build foot traffic and, therefore, interest in your company. Be sure, however, not to let the entertainment divert too much from the business at hand. Your magician or artist could work your product into his act.

681. When you're manning a trade show booth, always be sure to ask open-ended questions, like "What kind of industrial cleaner are you using now in your store?" or "What's the most frustrating thing about your current printer?" instead of questions that can be answered with a yes or no. Close-ended questions such as "Can I help you?" or "Are you looking for anything in particular today?" prevent the invitation that will frequently lead to lengthy, productive conversations.

682. Trade shows offer you a great opportunity to spot trends in product development and marketing ideas. Pick up your competitors' brochures, and make notes on new products and promotion ideas that catch your attention.

683. Get to the show an hour early to walk the floor to get ideas on the different types of exhibit displays that other companies are using.

684. Try to walk through the show during peak show hours in order to see which booths are drawing crowds. Take notice of the features that make these booths attract attention, and see which features you can incorporate into your display for future shows.

685. Entice people to your booth by calling attention to it before they even set foot in the exhibition hall. Have somebody hand out brochures to people at the entrance or to attendees as they're stepping off the busses.

686. Try exhibiting at a themed show that doesn't quite fit your target market. For example, a used-car dealer might think about exhibiting at a local home show. The advantage here is that there's likely to be no or very little competition in the field.

Following Up After the Show

687. After the show, contact the promoter to get a list of all of the people who did attend the show. Send these people a special postshow offer to entice them into doing business with your company.

688. After the show, send any requested information along with a personalized note, if appropriate, within one week. One study suggests that up to 80 percent of the leads generated at a trade show are never acted on, which means that you should have a captive audience to receive your message postshow.

689. Use the names you've collected at trade shows and fairs to keep customers informed of your promotions and activities. A potter from New York State who exhibits at around twenty shows from the beginning of May through mid-December sends each of the 1,500 names on his mailing list a calendar postcard that shows the full spectrum of the pottery he makes as well as the dates of his upcoming shows. He mails them out to his good customers twice a year, to let them know when he's going to be in their area.

WORKING WITH
CURRENT CUSTOMERS

You've probably heard it said that you'll get 80 percent of your business from 20 percent of your customers. There is a lot of truth to this statement, though a lot rides on how you treat your present customers.

Many times, the best marketing technique to use with current customers—and future ones as well—is to smile. People will hesitate to buy from you again if the experience they had during the transaction was unpleasant, even if you offer a product or service that is exclusive to your area or industry.

With this in mind, what follows is a slew of ideas that can enhance your business with customers on your present list, as well as with future ones, since your customers are quite likely to tell colleagues about your company and therefore provide you with plentiful word-of-mouth marketing—which is the best kind of all.

Creating Current Customers

690. Contrary to popular opinion, the customer is not always right. There are some bad customers out there who are nothing but trouble even though you may bend over backward to make them happy; you're better off not wasting your time. Focus instead on pursuing the majority of customers who have had good experiences with you.

691. Start to treat all your customers like family, whether that means taking the time to talk with them about their families, or giving them an extra something. If you'd do it for your own family, then you should do it for your customers.

692. Take advantage of the success that you've had with your current roster of customers by collecting all the testimonial letters that you've received, and either hang samples on the wall of your lobby or waiting area, or copy them and assemble them all in a looseleaf notebook to put in your waiting area.

693. You can ensure that a first-time customer will return to you again and again, and refer others to you, by giving her something for free after her first purchase. It can be expected, as in the case of a technician helping a customer make some minor adjustments to a car stereo, or unexpected, like sending a box of chocolates or flowers a week after you've made a major sale to a new customer.

694. Testimonials from previous customers—the more glowing and descriptive the better—can sometimes be the final bit of information a new customer needs about your business in order to become a regular customer.

695. In a retail outlet, you can get names for your mailing list by providing a simple fill-in-the-blank form. When you ask for the customer's name, address, and/or phone number, explain that this is a way for you to get them information about future sales. As a bonus for providing this information, you can offer them a coupon for 10 percent off their next purchase.

696. Some businesses make it a habit to ask their current customers for the names, addresses, and phone numbers of any friends who they think would like to receive information about your business. Some entrepreneurs think that this is too pushy, however, so use your best judgment.

Getting Information About Your Current Customers

697. A well-written customer survey can give you lots of valuable information and provide another source of names for a mailing list (although the inclusion of names and addresses in any survey should always be clearly optional).

698. If you design a customer survey, make sure that it is slanted more toward the customer than toward your business. For example, instead of asking your customers if they think you're a great place to shop, ask them instead if they think that they are getting their money's worth by shopping with you. Always ask the question in the second person; this will help elicit more direct and honest responses.

699. Hand out a questionnaire to departing guests with a discount coupon and a SASE. You can ask them the standard marketing questions, like where they heard about you, if they enjoyed their experience with you, as well as asking open-ended questions about what products or services they'd like to see you offer in the future. Make sure to put a stamp on the envelope or self-mailing questionnaire. This will earn brownie points.

700. In order to increase the responses to your survey, offer your customers a discount on their next purchase, a free gift, or the chance to win a more costly item in a drawing.

701. Before you introduce a new product or service as well as afterward, ask your customers what they really think of it and how you could make it better.

702. Whenever you are in contact with a current customer, always offer him the opportunity to provide you with feedback about your company. Sometimes, you can use this information to develop new avenues for your business.

703. If you want to do some market research on a new product or service while also cultivating the trust and business of your regular customers, consider including them in a limited test of your new item. For instance, one supermarket selected sixty of its best customers and offered them the opportunity to participate in an electronic grocery service. Customers got to try the service and offer their criticism to the company. In this way, they became even better customers, in part because the supermarket took their needs seriously.

704. Send the good customers on your list a special time-limited offer, which they can transfer to a friend if they are unable to take advantage of it.

705. Sign some of your best customers up for a one-year subscription to a magazine that concerns their work or lifestyle. This way, whenever they receive an issue, they'll think of you.

706. Show your customers that you respect them and their personal desires by developing a call cycle where you can determine how they prefer being contacted and how often. Says David Fickes of Advice Marketing, "Some people like to be called and then faxed, while others want you to fax and then call the next day. Some people just want E-mail while others want to be contacted only when we are representing new products."

707. Put yourself into your customers' shoes: approach your competition in the guise of a potential customer. Ask the kinds of questions that your customers ask you. You can learn a lot about customer service and adopt any new ideas for your own business.

708. The next time you're away from your business, test how your own staff rates at customer service with a blind call. Disguise your voice and ask some questions, making both typical and unusual requests. Make the necessary adjustments to staff policy as a result of your research.

709. Whenever you hand out a questionnaire to customers, make sure there's a built-in way to ensure that you receive as many responses as possible. For instance, the director of a community school withheld payment from teachers until she received all of their students' questionnaires. This provides the teachers with a real incentive to make sure that students comply.

Marketing to Current Customers

710. Although many people think of marketing in terms of attracting new customers, you should always keep in mind that marketing in whatever form will also help to keep these customers coming back. As you know, repeat customers are the lifeblood of any business, and the best thing about loyal clients is the fact that getting them back incurs little additional marketing costs. They're already convinced of the merits of your business, and you don't need to spend time or money trying to sell them on it; however, the marketing you use to go after new customers will also be seen by present customers and serve as a reminder for them.

711. If at all possible, write all or most of your correspondence to customers by hand. Or have one of your staff members do it.

712. If you can track the different types of brands that your customers purchase, send out a postcard to appropriate customers whenever you're having a particular sale on that brand. It takes work, but it will make you seem like a thoughtful business owner.

713. Collect information about the sales patterns of your customers to use in future promotions. For instance, the Macon Christian Bookstore in Macon, Georgia, keeps track of the customers who purchase a specific author or recording artist. When a new book or album is released, the store sends out postcards to customers who had bought the previous books or albums. This idea can be expanded to include specific categories of books or albums, too.

714. Every piece of merchandise you sell, from clothing to greeting cards, should have the name of your company and contact information on it. This is especially important if you rely on distributors or retail outfits that may decide to discontinue your line and cut off contact from consumers who may want to do repeat business with you.

715. Offer your good customers the equivalent of a frequent flyer program, where you provide them with credits every time they make a purchase from you. Whether it's "buy one, get one free," or, as in the case of a laundromat, offering a free minibox of detergent to good customers, these seemingly small gestures show that you do appreciate your loyal customers.

716. If you own a retail shop, promote your products with the use of signs inside your store. The posters that many manufacturers supply to retailers can help establish your image as a local business that is national in scope, with the help of its suppliers. Be careful not to go overboard, however. Cluttered signage can actually scare customers away.

717. You may want to emphasize a different special each day with a daily blackboard display or outdoor sandwich board. One deli achieves this by offering something free with the purchase of a sandwich every day: a free soda, dessert, or bag of chips. Customers have to go in the store to find out what that day's special is, and once they're there, they order something, even if they don't particularly care for dessert.

718. Send reminder cards out to customers who haven't visited your business in a while, just as the dentist does.

719. To cultivate more sales from current customers, think about offering a product-oriented package patterned after Fruit of the Month club. Three Dog Bakery, a company that produces all-natural dog biscuits, promotes a Treat of the Month club, which costs $200 for the year. The founders of the company report that much to their surprise, it has turned into a hot seller.

720. Whenever you get new brochures printed up for your business, be sure to give copies to all your regular customers. Detailing all your products and services will reinforce your business in the minds of your customers and also alert them to any new offerings.

721. If you regularly send out monthly bills to your current customers, try to add a different line every month toward the bottom of the invoice that spotlights a particular special sale or offer that's good for a limited time only.

722. You can reinforce the value of your product or service even as you're sending a bill: itemize and describe, in a positive, detailed way, exactly how you've been able to help your customer. For instance, a marketing specialist may state on the bill the response rate to a particular mailing or a personnel specialist can stress the number of successful placements in the last year.

Treating Your Customers Like Royalty

723. At holiday time in December, keep the name of your business in the minds of your best customers by sending them a unique gift. Give them the type of gift that you would give a favorite uncle or aunt: a gift certificate to a fancy mail-order business, an elegant gift basket filled with gourmet goodies, or for really good customers, a Mont Blanc pen.

724. Develop a way that your customers can share in the good fortune of your business. For instance, one automobile insurance company sends all its insured customers a dividend check for 20 percent of the premiums that they paid in the previous year on the anniversary date when they first joined up. And they do this even if you've filed a claim during the previous year.

725. If it's appropriate to your business, develop a detailed file on each customer that contains information about their occupations, children, hobbies, what they like to eat, how they pay for your service or business, or how often they buy from you. Then gear your marketing toward their interests. Send a handwritten letter, birthday and anniversary cards, Christmas cards, etc., that are as personalized as possible by including some of this information.

726. Impress your customers by using their names liberally throughout the course of any conversation with them. Make sure that your employees know to do this as well.

727. Send a special time-limited offer to your list of good customers, which they can transfer to a friend if they are unable to take advantage of it.

728. Whenever you spend time with a customer, try not to appear rushed or stressed. Make it seem as if you have all the time in the world for that customer. Arrange in advance to have an employee interrupt the meeting at a prescribed time, but make it seem as though this is beyond your control.

729. When sending out bills or invoices, it's important to include a line that conveys the fact that you appreciate the customer's business. Even though this may seem trite, the fact is that there are many businesses including this line in their bills, so if you don't, some customers may compare you unfavorably with other businesses that do.

730. If a current customer makes a referral to your business that results in a sale, reward that customer with a gift or discount coupon.

731. If you ever travel, or have contacts in other parts of the country, personally recommend other small businesses and attractions to your customers if you know that they will be traveling there in the near future. This is another way you can show your customers that you are treating them as more than a customer.

Keeping Your Customers Happy

732. Building goodwill among your customers entails not only refunding their money in case they're dissatisfied but also going further and replacing the item as well. Not every business owner can afford to do this, but if you apply it in certain circumstances, it's bound to create extremely loyal customers.

733. Send your customers a birthday card every year, in addition to a holiday card. Some companies go a step further and send birthday cards to every member of a good customer's family.

734. If a customer has to cancel an order with you, try this: Offer him a gift certificate that's worth twice the price of the order he just canceled. There's a double benefit to this. First, you don't have to pay back the money at a time when cash flow may already be tight, and second, since it's a gift, you're making a clear goodwill gesture to the customer. It ensures that the customer will come back, which affords you a chance to cultivate a repeat customer. One industry that does this with great effect is the innkeeping and bed-and-breakfast field.

735. If you don't operate in a retail storefront, make sure you make it very easy for customers to do business with you. This means accepting orders in any way possible: via the mail, fax, an 800 number, E-mail, or from your Web site. (There is some concern about the safety of sending credit card numbers by E-mail, but technology is currently addressing this issue.)

736. If you run a mail-order business or need to communicate with your customers through the mail, consider using a delivery service that offers tracking abilities to both you and your customers. Lots of consumers are going online to check the status of their orders, and you can also do so to tell a customer the exact date of delivery. Tracking orders will help you save money since you won't have to replace lost orders.

737. Once you've done business with a customer, offer her financing and credit terms. This will mean extra bookkeeping, but it will also lead to increased revenues.

738. Keep your customers happy with an occasional bonus. If you send out monthly invoices, for instance, surprise them every few months by giving a 10 percent discount on that month's bill. They'll stick around just to see what you'll do for them next.

739. One of the most important things you can do to grow your business is to develop a well thought-out game plan for how your company is going to follow up on inquiries from both new and current customers. Some entrepreneurs have a form letter they automatically send out at a given period of time after the initial contact, while others make a quick phone call. With E-mail becoming more and more pervasive, you may want to look into this form of communication, which is the most efficient way of keeping in touch.

740. When your customers start to leave after making a purchase, always ask them if there was something else you would have done that would have improved their experience.

741. If you hear that someone has had a less than stellar experience with your business, bend over backward to alleviate it. Don't just ignore it. You're probably familiar with the old adage that if someone is happy with your company, he won't tell anyone about it, but if he has had a bad experience, he'll tell everybody he knows. If you do everything that you can to make it up to him, he may not brag about your actions to his friends, but then again, he won't be bad-mouthing you either. And you'll probably have a customer for life.

742. More isn't necessarily better when it comes to marketing your business. "Many people have the mistaken notion that they have to write more letters or make more sales calls to get more business," says Andrew Morrison of Nia Direct, a marketing consulting firm. "What you really need to realize is if you start with the clients you have, you can grow your business from within. You don't need hundreds of clients; instead, you should focus on a couple of clients that are extremely large, and then if your business works for them, you get larger budgets next year to expand it."

Keeping Track of Your Current Customers

743. From the first day that you're in business, keep track of the names and addresses and other contact information for every customer who walks through your door or calls on the phone. You will build a terrific mailing list.

744. You can customize a commercially available database program such as FileMaker or Microsoft Exchange in order to keep track of the past purchases your customers have made from you. You can extract information from your cash register receipts and inventory lists in order to create personalized profiles of each of your customers. Then, the next time they visit your business or call you, you can alert them to a new product or service they should be interested in, based on the records you keep.

745. If your business is service oriented, send out confirmation letters the same day that you iron out the details on a new project with a customer. The loyalty of long-term customers is built on your promptness and consideration.

746. If you offer a product or service that may be revised or updated periodically, be sure to have each customer register with you. You can keep them updated on new versions and offer them other products and services in which they may be interested.

WORKING THE PHONES

The telephone can be one of the most powerful tools you can use to market your business. Whether it's to alert a special customer to a limited-time offer or to call a prospective customer who's visited your business but has never made a purchase, a phone call can mean the difference between a successful business and just getting by.

But care should be taken when using the phone to market your business, since so many people are becoming increasingly hostile to having the peace and quiet of their homes interrupted by yet another business calling them to try to sell them something. Use these tips to promote and temper your phone marketing plan—which every business should use in one form or another—and that personalized touch can help your business grow by leaps and bounds. Generally, the most effective telephone sales techniques offer specials to new and current customers, advise customers of upcoming promotions, and alert customers to last-minute or limited additions to your existing product line.

Getting Ready

747. Vow to strike *ers*, *ums*, and other gruntlike noises that fill the pauses in your speech. We all do it, but when it comes from an authority figure—like you're supposed to be in representing your business—it lessens the effectiveness of your oral presentation.

748. If you're planning to do some telephone soliciting and have a script already written, before you make one phone call to a prospect, tape yourself reciting a typical exchange. Then play it back—or have someone else listen to it—so that you can catch what does and doesn't work.

749. If you're a one-person business, get into the habit of speaking in the first person plural whenever you're talking with a current or potential customer. This helps to create the impression that you have the manpower to do the job.

750. If you're making cold calls to promote your business, make sure that your timing is right. For instance, if you're selling a product or service that tends to be purchased most often at a particular time of year such as a lawn care system or device, make sure that you make the calls no more than a month in advance, or a week after the optimum time.

751. Whenever writing a script or outline to use in a phone solicitation, make sure that more than 50 percent of your sentences are in the form of questions. And make sure that most of these questions are open-ended instead of requiring just a yes or no answer.

752. When you are marketing your business to other businesses, start with businesses listed in the Yellow Pages that you think might be able to use your products or services.

Sales Calls

753. Hire a commissioned salesperson to call people who have requested information about your business in the past but haven't yet become customers.

754. After an initial phone call, if a prospect is interested in what you have to offer, he or she may give detailed instructions on what you should do next. The good news is that if you do exactly what he says, then you'll stand out, since most cold callers never customize their follow-ups to the prospect's desires. This means that if he wants a one-page proposal in the form of a fax, get it out to her right away.

755. "Mr. Douglas told me to call." One of the most effective ways to get a stranger to listen to your sales pitch is if you can name a mutual acquaintance who referred you.

756. If a prospect has asked you to send more information in response to a phone call, send it out immediately and on the envelope itself, write "Thanks for your time.

Enclosed is the information you requested during our phone call."

757. If you have a number of your employees working on telephone solicitations at the same time, arrange to have some kind of reward system set in place whenever a sale is made. This could be an old-fashioned school bell that gets rung throughout the office, or a ticket to a concert or sports event that is given to the staffer who has made the most sales that day. Even if you have employees who aren't working full-time at telephone sales, these techniques can still work wonders.

758. If you regularly call customers to let them know about a new product or service, be sure to offer them special deals on your products that have been around for a while as well. After all, there are a large number of customers who never buy the first edition of anything.

759. If you run a mail-order business where the majority of your sales come in over the phone, prepare your order takers to upsell; that is, to try to sell the customer an additional item as long as she is on the phone. Rather viewing this as an intrusion, many customers appreciate being given additional information.

760. Make follow-up calls to people who have written for information about your business but who have never become your customers. Ask them why they never responded to your initial mailing, and invite them to participate now with a special incentive. It could be that your brochure or ad has actually been stuck on their refrigerator for more than a year, and that they're just waiting for a good reason to respond.

761. The first thing you should do whenever you call a potential customer on the phone is to ask if they have a few minutes now. If they say that they're in the middle of something, ask when a better time to call back would be, and then do it. They'll be more likely to listen to your pitch later if you've shown that you respect their time.

762. When calling any prospect, state your name, your purpose, and your pitch. Then let the other person speak. Many sales reps end up talking too much when trying to sell something. The best thing you can do is to listen and ask pertinent questions.

763. When calling customers who have purchased from you in the past, briefly mention an item about their last order, and then explain why it's time for you to do business again.

764. Whenever you leave a voice-mail message for someone you don't know, try not to act overly familiar. Cute asides and forced comments that the caller is presuming may be offensive.

765. When you leave a voice-mail message, whether you know the person or not, be professional, give your name and your business clearly and slowly, taking the time to spell it, and state the nature of your call. Be sure to repeat your telephone number at the end of the message.

766. Whenever you're talking on the phone with a potential customer, always ask if the person has any more questions. This gives him a chance to address any issues that your questions haven't covered.

767. If your type of business is not generally known for cold-calling, then give it a try.

768. Spend time with prospective customers on the phone—as much time as they want and need. Though you might find yourself having to make small talk, the fact that you are taking extra time with a potential customer will stand out in a lot of people's minds.

769. Whenever talking with a customer on the phone, make sure that the person on the other end knows that you're still on the phone. The best way to do this is with short *um-hmmms* or *yesses* or *nos*. Long pauses and the lack of a response will send the message that you're distracted and that what your customer has to say really isn't that important.

Checking In by Phone

770. Call customers about a week after they've made a purchase from you to check in and see how they're doing with it. This is particularly important with major items such as cars or computer systems.

771. Think of all the good intentions you've had in the last year that have fallen by the wayside because you're simply too busy. Your potential customers are in the same boat, so once you've made an initial contact with them, if they're familiar with your business, the next step is to get them on the phone within a week or two after your first mailing. In lieu of a phone call, send a postcard with a personal note.

772. Whenever making follow-up calls to customers, make sure that you keep accurate records of whom you talked to, on what date, as well as what you discussed. Also make note of any follow-up action that you took. This way you have a history to draw on when making future calls.

Uncrossing the Wires: The Technical Side

773. Busy signals in any business can sink your business quicker than anything else. Add extra lines if possible, install voice mail that picks up whenever a line is in use, or get call forwarding.

774. One of the most important things you can do to ensure that callers don't spend too much time on hold is to have the employee who picks up take their name and number and tell them she will call back if it looks as if they'll be on hold for more than thirty seconds. Most callers will appreciate this courtesy.

775. Set up a hot line that customers can call any day or night to get more information about your company. With freestanding voice-mail machines, this is easy to do. A fax on demand program can serve the same purpose.

776. Make sure that your phone is answered promptly and in a friendly manner.

777. If you have to put people on hold, make sure that you don't let them languish there for more than thirty seconds without checking in with them. This is an easy way to lose new business.

778. In a local computer store, taped to every salesperson's phone is the message: E-mail first, fax second, the phone is your last resort. E-mail and faxes are much more efficient, and more respectful of your customers' time than the phone. Therefore, if you can follow this rule, you will likely be rewarded with more customers.

779. When your customers call in to your business and are put on hold, what are they hearing? Silence is the worst thing next to a hard-sell message. The kind of music you choose to play to callers on hold basically will depend on who your market is. Upscale businesses gravitate toward classical music, while youth-oriented clothing shops prefer to play a simulcast of the local Top 40 station.

780. Provide a discount of 5 percent to callers who have been on hold more than a minute by announcing this benefit during your on-hold message.

781. If you can invest in technology that tells callers how long they should expect to remain on hold, or if they're the next caller to be helped, this will help soothe impatient customers.

782. What does your answering machine play? Have fun with music, voices, sound effects, and anything else you can think of. Many businesses these days are using their on-hold phone features as a hard-sell ad for their businesses. You'll get more attention by showing your creativity: One B&B in upstate New York has "Holiday Inn" as its theme.

783. If you run a small business that's not oriented toward mail order, instruct all employees to pick up the phone if it rings more than three times.

800 and 888 Toll-Free Numbers

784. Get an 800 number. You'll find that it makes a huge difference in your customer response rate, especially if the majority of your customers come from outside your area.

785. Many entrepreneurs scramble to make their 800 numbers spell out something that is relevant to their businesses. However, this can backfire on you because people tend to believe that they will remember your number, when the truth is that if they don't write it down, most people will not remember it.

786. Like fax machines, 800 and 888 numbers are an ubiquitous tool in business today no matter what the product or service.

Other Ideas

787. If you can, accept orders through your fax machine, if most of your customers send in their orders on an order form. It's quicker and easier than calling up an order hot line.

788. If you're interested in using a 900 number to market your business, make sure that you are offering information or advice that the caller feels is worth the dollar or two a minute he is paying for the service. Try to change the message at least once a week to facilitate repeat business.

789. Make sure that your voice-mail messages are constantly updated with news of sales or other special promotions that you're running. A surprising number of calls do come in after hours, so you can keep marketing your business even when you're not around.

790. If you want to distribute thousands of free samples to your target audience, do it with a 900 number. Offer the specific option of learning more about your company on the phone with voice-mail options, and make it easy for callers to leave their names and addresses. Make sure the dollar value of the sample is worth the call, however.

791. A 900 number is a great way to build your mailing list; running a contest or sweepstakes will generate many entries from new prospects.

792. Marketing consultant Tom Feltenstein believes that most businesses overlook the marketing they could be aiming at other local businesses. Feltenstein suggests that you make eight or ten calls to local businesses each week.

793. One rule of thumb when it comes to not turning your customers off with too many phone calls is to make sure that you call them no more than every three months. And of course, be sure that you do not call them more than once to offer them the same product.

794. Sometimes, the best way to get through to the person you really want to speak to is to call before or after hours. Secretaries and assistants tend to work nine to five, but executives and presidents usually don't.

795. When it comes to voice mail, many people choose to let their voice mail serve as their secretary. To circumvent this, always press 0, and ask that the person you are trying to reach be paged. Or you can explain the reason for your call to the operator and ask her to pass along a personal note to the person. Your prospect may be more receptive to your message if it's coming from another staff member and not from you.

796. Whenever talking on the phone to a customer, be sure to smile. After all, the caller will be able to tell if you're not.

797. Your business hours may be nine to five or slightly longer, but you should be aware that many of your customers will call after you've gone home. An answering service usually isn't sufficient, nor is a machine, so you might want to put call forwarding on and hire someone for the evening to take the calls in his home.

798. When speaking with customers and potential customers on the phone, be animated, but not hyper.

799. If you don't have a good phone manner but want to explore telephone sales for your business, assign the task to one of your employees and offer bonuses and incentives for success.

800. Every day, call up five of your best customers from the past year and tell them about a special that you're offering only to them and only today. Of course, you need a pretty sizable customer list to do this, but direct contact from the owner or manager of your business, as well as the feeling that they're getting something that everyone else isn't, will add to their loyalty.

YOU ARE YOUR OWN BEST MARKETING TOOL

Even if your product or service is the best or only one around for miles, if you are not responsive to your own customers, you will lose business. Twenty-four hours a day, no matter where you go or what you're doing, you are essentially serving as a walking billboard for your business.

So make the most of it. Realize that your own role as your business's best marketing tool can be fun and fulfilling at the same time.

Customer Service

801. When you become the best source of information for consumers, they will become your customers. Sims, the discount clothing retailer, uses as its motto, "An educated consumer is our best customer." Take the time to teach consumers about your business whether they call on the phone or walk in off the street.

802. The Miracle on Thirty-fourth Street: Always refer customers to other area businesses if you are unable to help them. (But first take down their name, address, and phone number and send them a handwritten note expressing your hope that they found satisfaction, and extend an invitation to do business with you in the future.)

803. If your storefront business attracts a lot of tourists or out-of-towners, buy a large map of your neighborhood or town for your office walls and pinpoint the location of your property. Also mark the location of nearby retail stores, offices, hospitals, funeral homes, factories, schools, recreational facilities, and other businesses in the area that your customers may be trying to find.

Networking

804. Wear your name tag at any business event where potential customers, suppliers, or competitors are likely to be in attendance. Your name tag could even be embellished with a stick-on graphic (a star or decal) to make sure people look at your tag and remember you.

805. Make it a habit to write down the names and businesses of people you meet if you think you can do business with them in the future, or ask for their business cards.

806. Get to know the secretaries at the businesses you're trying to attract. Secretaries and assistants usually know most of what is going on at a particular company and, if they decide they want to help you, they can serve as a valuable contact.

807. If you network with other area businesspeople, you might want to consider publishing a regular newsletter every two to three months that you can use to help local businesspeople coordinate their efforts and projects aimed at attracting new customers.

808. Whenever speaking in public, whether it's one-on-one to a customer or to a roomful of a thousand, keep an eye on your body language. Too much, and it will detract from your message; too little, and you look stiff.

809. Whenever talking with someone who can either help you to promote your business or a current or prospective customer, speak as if the sale and agreement is a done deal. Your inherent confidence will in turn make the customer feel more confident about doing business with you.

810. Make a photo of your product into a button or badge that you can wear wherever you go.

811. If you want to get information from your competitors who are located outside your immediate territory, offer to tell them exactly what has worked for you. You may wind up working cooperatively to both your benefits.

812. A lawyer who became a professional clown—no joke!—publicized his services by attending fairs and festivals. He'd show up in full costume, joke with whomever walked by, and handed out business cards. His first jobs resulted from those appearances where he now performs—and gets paid for it.

813. A nightclub promoter wanted to pack his place with warm bodies, so he approached people who work in people-oriented businesses. He gave free passes to hairstylists and clothing salespeople at local stores and encouraged them to talk up the club among their clientele. Within a month, the club was packed every night and it became the place to be seen in the area.

814. It's easy to fall into a rut if you've been in business for a while. Find out about the marketing that other businesses are doing by holding a regular brainstorming dinner meeting—either in a restaurant or a potluck—that meets regularly, with no more than five or six participants from both competing and complementary businesses in your area to keep it manageable. Have everyone write down one marketing idea and put the papers in a hat. Pass the hat, pick one, and go do it. Report on the results at the next meeting.

815. If you are shy, or do not fare well at social gatherings, ask one of your staff members to go in your place. The opportunity to meet with other businesspeople is too valuable to let it slip away. It may be just the boost you need for your business and good for your staff member who'd relish this opportunity.

816. If you belong to a Chamber of Commerce and feel that your business is not receiving the number of referrals that you consider fair, the answer is to become involved in the various committees that the Chamber has to offer. This will not only provide you the opportunity to give advice about important business decisions for your town or city but also make your name and face familiar to the Chamber staff who are in charge of making all referrals to customers.

817. If you're looking to run your business from an outside office and live in an urban area, consider renting space from a business incubator. Incubators are large office suites with separate, usually small, offices that house entrepreneurs who are just getting their businesses off the ground. While you can get emotional support from other entrepreneurs, it's also a great way to network for new business.

818. If you're not a particularly social person but still feel as though you need to attend local business networking events, bring a friend with you. It will be easier to be introduced to other people.

819. Join the Chamber of Commerce. Most Chambers hold monthly gatherings that give all the Chamber members a chance to mix with other businesspeople in the area and, more important, to work with other business owners. These mixers will provide you with two very important opportunities: (1) you'll be able to meet other entrepreneurs in a nonbusiness environment and (2) you'll get business referrals from these professional contacts.

820. The next time you go to a party or trade event, spend at least half your time eavesdropping. Frequently somebody will let some information drop as a way to impress the listener and therefore result in your best tips for future expansion in your own business.

821. One effective way to network with your competitors is to inform them whenever you have been stiffed by a customer. This will alert them to be wary of future dealings with this customer, and it will also help to open up lines of communication between you and them.

822. Start your own local association of entrepreneurs. Invite people from all kinds of businesses and make it a point to meet once a month to brainstorm on cooperative marketing opportunities.

823. Wherever you are, open your mouth about your business. One real estate broker was doing business at his bank's drive-through window, and when the teller took her deposit, he asked her if she was interested in buying a house. She said she was, he gave her his business card, and she ended up buying a town house from him.

824. If you don't have a partner whom you can bounce ideas off, marketing or otherwise, find someone in your field who can make herself available for you. She doesn't need to know more about your product or service than you do, but a critical eye definitely helps. "You need another person working with you who understands just enough to be critical, and yet doesn't know it all so can ask the silly questions that make all the difference," says David Fickes of Advice Marketing. "Because if you can't talk them into it, you ought to have a hard time talking anyone else into it."

Getting New Business

825. If you leave your nine-to-five job to start your own business and plan to sign up your employer as your main client, don't count the chickens yet . . . Rob Epp, one of the owners of Willow New Media, a software development firm in Norwalk, Connecticut, says that he expected that "the companies we were working for would sign us up and give us the work once we started out on our own. That's not how companies work. Very often you leave a company and become persona non grata for a while. Then, after a lot of hard work and networking, they may turn out to become very good customers."

826. Place signs for your business on your personal car as well as your company vehicles.

827. Fax broadcasting can be quite effective when targeting business-to-business clients. Like direct-mail houses, there are several companies that specialize in sending faxes to a targeted group of businesses. You supply the copy, and the fax company sends it out to the businesses that you've targeted.

828. Send an advertising specialty—key chain, pen, refrigerator magnet, or the like—to prospective customers, not past or current ones, to introduce them to your business.

829. Identify your customers' needs and personalize your marketing efforts accordingly: for instance, a landscaper can send letters and brochures to those homes in a particular neighborhood where the lawns and gardens need attention. Avoid negative comments as you play up the ways in which you could help make improvements simply and economically.

830. If your business relies on traffic from tourists to some degree, it may be worth your while to place brochures and other marketing materials with your local tourist information office, the Chamber of Commerce, or at local businesses such as diners and gas stations, which often have space to place brochures for local attractions. For instance: one new bed-and-breakfast owner in a tourist-oriented town brought a basket of freshly baked muffins to the town's Chamber of Commerce every day for a month during the height of tourist season. He attached a card with the name, address, and telephone number of his business to the basket. When tourists came into the office for recommendations, they ate the muffins, saw the card, and made enquiries. The B&B had more business than it could handle for the rest of the season.

831. If you're selling your product to other businesses, either for their own use or for them to resell, be sure to ask them many detailed questions to determine what they need for their businesses.

832. Offer to start out with a small project with a new client; many times, the good work you do on this project can be your best marketing tool.

833. Investigate catalog sales, not only as a way to move more product but also as a way to build awareness among consumers who may end up buying the product directly from you. Especially if you place one of your products in a nationally distributed catalog, this means that millions of people across the country will first hear about your product and company through the catalog. Then later on, when they hear about you somewhere else, they are more likely to respond.

834. One great way to engender loyalty among a brand-new base of customers is to head for the largest company in your town or area and hand out discount cards to every employee, which they can use whenever they make a purchase from you no matter how insignificant.

835. Sometimes, wining and dining a potential customer is still the best way to market your business. If you don't have the money to spare, you can still woo the client if you belong to a business barter group. Barter exchanges enable you to build up credits that you can then use to trade for services and/or products with other business members of the exchange—like restaurants.

836. The best way to attract new customers to your business is by going after people who are unhappy with the way a competitor of yours has treated them. According to a study by the Research Institute of America, 68 percent of customers who stop patronizing a business do so because they feel that a business doesn't care about them. Therefore, you should always provide the best service you can to your customers while pursuing the more than two-thirds of possible customers who believe they have been treated with indifference from a competitor. One way to find them is to run ads that ask people if they're unhappy with their current supplier, and then offer your business as an alternative.

837. If you're pursuing wholesale markets as a regular source of revenue for your business, don't stint on the free samples. Staci Munic Mintz, who runs Little Miss Muffin, a Chicago-based company specializing in healthy baked goods, brings in an incredibly generous box of muffins for the owners and managers of cafés and espresso bars to try.

838. The next time a local or regional publication comes out with a list of the top 100 employers and/or businesses in your area, make a point to send each one sales material about your company where appropriate.

839. One frequently overlooked source of new customers is your own suppliers. After all, they have customers who are also entrepreneurs just like you. So ask the supplier to ask his other customers if they need your service or product before you call. Many suppliers will be happy to do this, since it is a way of winning brownie points.

840. If you are looking to get business from a local retailer, try to stop by frequently just to show your face.

You don't need to ask for work; instead, you should ask how things are, including how their business is doing, and just chat.

841. Think about what types of groups and associations would benefit from your product or service. Contact the marketing director or the membership chairperson of these groups to offer your product or service at a discount to its members. If you can convince them to offer a product as an automatic membership benefit, you'll increase the prospects for your other products or services.

Growing Your Business

842. If you work with a distributor or wholesaler that handles all or part of your sales for you, keep in frequent contact by phone, mail, and in person. Distributors and wholesalers frequently handle hundreds, if not thousands, of other clients, so it's vitally important to make you and your products visible to them.

843. Whether you sell a product or service, sometimes shedding a little light on the history of your business will help to build interest in your business and, therefore, sales. In fact, this can be a cornerstone of an effective marketing and advertising plan and show customers that you have a strong track record.

844. Publicly make a forecast or predict a trend concerning your industry. You can either make it the cornerstone of your marketing campaign or offer it up as a challenge to your competitors.

845. If you're looking to market your business in a foreign country, your best bet is to hire a native of that country to do the work. Many people in foreign countries are skeptical of Americans who come in to market a product to them, even though they might want to buy it. Hiring a native means that there is a level of trust from the beginning.

846. You can build a good customer base by promoting yourself to others who are in the same line that you are. For instance, if you're running a home-based business, no matter what line you're in, try seeing other home-based business owners as an additional market.

847. If you are wholesaling your product to retail accounts, you have to go to the people who really make the decisions about placement of your product in the store. Determine who's in charge of deciding where your product is displayed. Networking with the front-line people can be as effective, if not more so, than schmoozing the executive buyers.

848. Some product-oriented businesses may be able to increase revenues substantially with even a small, well-placed storefront. Mark Beckloff and Dan Dye of the Three Dog Bakery in Kansas City outgrew their home base after the first six months in business. They rented a tiny storefront. The business began to take off to the point where it grossed one million dollars in 1995.

Cooperative Marketing

849. Work with a complementary business to place your respective business cards or brochures in each other's customer's packages. This is especially effective if you're offering a product or service that will enhance the value of the purchase they've just made from the cooperating business.

850. Contact appropriate businesses within a ten-mile radius of your business, and provide them with brochures about your company so they can recommend your product or service to their customers. Of course, offer to do the same thing for your customers, accepting their brochures or business cards and displaying them prominently at your place of business.

851. Form a local association of other small businesses in your industry to meet once a month for social and business matters. Generate a round-robin fax or phone circle each month or every couple of weeks to circulate news and/or leads. Every few months, promote your membership as a whole by sending a press release about the association, along with a brochure or directory of all the members, if warranted.

852. If money for marketing is tight, look to creative barter arrangements. One woman, a handwriting analyst, wanted to join a local club because she liked to swim. She made a deal with the social director that, in exchange for a membership, she would talk about the art of handwriting analysis with the members of the club one hour a week. Some of those club members who belonged to other clubs invited her to speak at their clubs as well. She also gained a handful of individual clients who wanted her to analyze their own handwriting.

853. Want "free" display space? A florist persuaded the director of a local mall to let her arrange a floral display in the middle of the mall to promote her business to both wholesale and retail customers for one weekend. She then sent out invitations to potential clients, such as hotels, for a special breakfast that she arranged before the mall opened. She also frequently trades with bridal shows by decorating their main entrance with flowers in exchange for a booth.

854. If your business relies on tourist traffic to some extent, it's a good idea to get together with other area businesses to offer a package deal to visitors. For instance, a motel may want to arrange a deal with admission-only attractions around town for free passes to give out to guests, which appeals to a particular group of people who want to be told what to do and where to go.

855. Is there another business in town that appeals to a super-specialized audience? It's easy to promote yourself in connection with it. For example, if there's a special museum in town that regularly draws travelers, arrange with the museum to place your brochure in the lobby and also to do co-op mailings and share postage costs whenever they send their brochure out to people who request it. Consider contacting any clubs or publications that also specialize in the same field and offer a discount or special promotion that ties in.

856. Team up with a well-known local or regional manufacturer so you can offer a sample of your product or service as a premium; you know, two UPC labels and a buck for handling to receive this five-dollar value.

857. Think of the package deals you can offer with other businesses in town that have an audience that overlaps with yours. For instance, a restaurant with a special two-for-one meal can get together with a motel that offers a discount on the second night, combined with a local museum that adds discounted admissions. The combinations that you will be able to come up with are endless.

Common Sense

858. When you're dealing face-to-face with customers, suppliers, associates, and even competitors, make eye contact. It's a simple matter of conveying your own trustworthiness and confidence as well as displaying interest in the other person.

859. If you're selling a service through in-person sales appointments, make sure that the way you dress matches what it is you're trying to sell. For instance, if you run a housecleaning service, don't show up in a suit and tie or a fancy dress that looks as if it only gets worn on Sundays for church. Customers expect to see service people in uniforms, but even a chimney sweep should be neat and tidy. Make your potential customers feel comfortable and confident in you.

860. Stay alert to new developments in your community. This way, you can find out what concerns people most in your community and use this information to mold future products and services.

861. Many small-business owners credit "word of mouth" as being the most effective marketing technique for their businesses. But how does it work? Stephan Schiffman, the author of a number of books about marketing, says "The best way to capitalize on word of mouth marketing is probably to tell everyone you meet what you do for a living."

862. Good ideas for marketing your product or service can come from the most unlikely sources: the local librarian, your next-door neighbor, or even the policeman on your beat. These are people with networks of their own in the community who often know what's really going on in town.

Doing Good

863. You can win a lot of attention on a yearly basis by sponsoring a "citizenship" award for the one person who has made a difference by doing good for their community.

864. You can also give an annual award for the individual or business in your field that has done the most to enhance the image of the industry.

865. Charge a flat fee, open up your doors—or rent space at a local community center—and hold a day-long or night-long event where all proceeds are donated to a local charity that the community is sympathetic toward. Any kind of business can do this for any reason.

866. If there is a tragedy in your area, one way to help out is by donating goods or services from your business to the people affected. Being a good corporate citizen by making donations in times of need and/or during seasonal fund-raising drives for the United Way means that you will probably receive some press coverage for your efforts just by the fact that you helped.

867. If a long-term community project—like a house building by Habitat for Humanity—is taking place in your neighborhood, donate food or materials for the workers at regular intervals.

868. Promote a program where your business donates a free computer to the local school once students and parents can present you with more than $50,000 worth of receipts from your business.

869. If community sports are big in your community, you should strongly consider sponsoring a team. In exchange, you'll receive exposure, goodwill, and a probable increase in business.

870. If you are looking for something for your business to sponsor and want something more than a Little League team to help your name stand out, consider starting an annual running race and donate all proceeds to local community organizations. Though it's initially a lot of work, you can usually convince other business owners to come help and share the cost and the work, though with you acting as the founding sponsor, the name of your business can always get top billing.

871. If you have incorporated some environmentally friendly aspects into your business recently, be sure to publicize this fact. Even though many environmental stories may be rehashes, a business that pays attention to ecological issues is likely to get some press for their efforts. Your efforts will not only save you money, but also gain the approval of both customers and the press, which will result in increased business.

872. Let your business serve as a permanent drop-off location for the Salvation Army or local food bank.

873. If you run a retail store and can spare the space, one of the most effective services you can supply to your customers, especially if the majority of them are young mothers, is a play space where children can be kept occupied while their parents are shopping, but are still visible from any place in the store.

874. If you're in a service business, and you have more work than you know what to do with, if a new project comes in, don't automatically accept it. By overextending yourself, you run the risk of doing a poor job, which can go a long way toward negating any marketing you do in the future. Instead, pass it along to a colleague or outsource it to a freelancer. You'll win brownie points all around.

875. If you're in the business of selling a product that frequently wears out or needs to be replaced, like clothing or books, design a campaign where people can bring in their old clothing or books, get a discount from you on any new purchases, and you can give the donated merchandise to a charity. Either you or your customers can get the tax deduction.

876. Let the local high school band use your venue for bake sales and car washes to raise money for their trip to Washington, D.C. You'll get lots of free publicity.

877. Small-business people who show that they're socially responsible in some way, either by employing disabled or "unemployable" people or by donating a percentage of their profit to a nonprofit organization, will gain the attention of both customers and the media. This will show that you're interested in being a good corporate citizen every day of the week, and not just for special events in the community.

878. Your local newspaper and TV and radio stations are required to run a certain amount of programming to improve the public good. You can take advantage of this forum to promote your point of view and your business. For example, if a new piece of legislation has altered the way you do business, for better or worse, contact your local TV or radio station about going on the air to say what you think about it. Public-affairs programming can either be a brief segment with you speaking into the camera or participating in a weekly talk show with other panelists and an interviewer. In either case, it's good exposure for you and your business.

879. One great way to portray your business as an upstanding member of the community is to give a prize to a resident whose talent somehow ties in with your business. For instance, a new-car dealer could hold a contest for the best example of a particular classic car, or a local restaurant could hand out a prize to the best cook at a local church fair.

880. By donating a portion of your profits to a nonprofit organization or other charity, your customers can deduct the portion that you are contributing from their own taxes.

881. Display a community bulletin board in your store that people can use to publicize Boy Scout car washes, school plays, or church suppers. Put it on a wall near the back of your store so that people will have to walk through your entire store in order to get to it.

882. Donate one of your products or services to the annual local public TV or radio auction. Then make up a sign or press release that says "As seen on . . ." You'll get lots of free promotion on the air, and your participation will ensure that present and potential customers know that you and your business care about more than just making money.

883. If you run your business from a regular office space, offer the use of your office as a meeting space to local nonprofit groups for free. They tend to remember largesse and will send lots of future business to you, not your competitors. It'll cost you next to nothing. Be sure to place your business card or other promotional materials at the door so that participants can take them on the way out.

884. Church groups and service clubs are always looking for speakers for monthly meetings. Your best bet is to arrange to speak at a club luncheon in an area that has the potential to bring you lots of business. The topic? What it's like to run your own business. Hand out your brochure with a discount coupon applicable toward their visit at the end of your talk.

885. Make it a point to regularly volunteer your time to local charities and community activities. If you absolutely can't find the time, either allow one of your employees to volunteer on company time, or arrange to donate your business products or services to the organization. For instance, animal shelters always have wish lists of things that they need in order to keep running smoothly. This could be anything from a case of paper towels to a used copy machine.

886. Get involved and get your name out into the community by serving on the boards of local nonprofit organizations, the school board, or other councils. The other members will be impressed that you care enough to make the time and may indeed send some business your way in the future.

887. You can effectively promote your name and business by running for a local elective office.

888. Get involved in your community as a volunteer or member of the board of the Chamber of Commerce or the regional association for your field. You'll help yourself and your business become more visible.

UNIQUE IDEAS

As a small-business owner, you have two big advantages over the big guys: speed and innovation. Many times, a marketing idea at a big corporation has to be sliced and diced by hundreds of people before it is able to see the light of day. By that time, it's usually become so bland as to be ineffective for attracting attention. Needless to say, this big company procedure also takes an inordinate amount of time.

But the way you market your business is different. You're small enough to be able to come up with an idea and to have it in place the same day. You can be outrageous or refined, depending on your mood and what you want to accomplish.

Consider some of the following ideas as a way to gain attention for your business. Certainly you can come up with some of your own unique ideas as well.

Introducing Your Product to Market

889. A celebrity endorsement—for which you'll likely have to pay—may be an appropriate way to launch your product. Once you're established, especially with a solid repeat business, you can spend your marketing dollars in other ways . . . but you'll have the benefit of the association with a celebrity for a long time.

890. If you can name one of your products or services after a more familiar national brand name without infringing on it, you'll get a lot of free mileage. You can also choose names that reflect programs used by local non-profits to help get your message out.

891. Time the introduction of a new product or service to the appropriate season. For instance, if your new service is geared toward new college graduates who are looking for their first jobs, wait until May or June to promote it. Bridal products are traditionally introduced in January or February and back-to-school promotions take place in August.

892. If you're thinking of renaming your business, or choosing a name for a new branch of your company, consider using the letter *A* as the first letter of the name. When you appear in the Yellow Pages, yours will be the first listing. Many entrepreneurs who have chosen this route report that their Yellow Page sales have increased almost 100 percent in some cases.

893. Premium sales can be your business's best friend when it comes to getting your business off the ground. Jim Hoskins of Maximum Press published his first book, about an IBM software package, only after he received a commitment from IBM to buy a certain number of books to give away to their customers. "Their commitment alone was enough to make the book profitable," says Hoskins. He published a few books in this way, building his business to the point where he could afford to publish the books he really wanted to publish.

894. You know the old adage "You can't get a job without experience, but you can't get experience without a job"? The same applies if you are running your own business. Especially in artistic fields, like interior design, many fledgling entrepreneurs often do their first job for free so people will hear about them.

Selling Your Product

895. Can a few of your products be sold through a vending machine? Especially if they're products not usually sold through these machines, this may be a good outlet for your business.

896. Contact the Home Shopping Network or QVC about the possibility of going on the air to sell your product. The more unusual the product, the better, but the tried and true will also find favor with the producers. Sending in a videotape that gives a taste of your personal energy and promotional talents will go a long way.

897. Even though the *Encyclopedia Britannica* has gone the way of the dinosaur, you can still sell some products well by going door to door, albeit to people you already know, or selling directly at local businesses and offices. For example, you can leave a sample of the product with the receptionist and then return a few days later to take orders. At the very least, you'll get some valuable and cheap market research done.

898. If you're considering handing out flyers to strangers on a street corner, give this old standby a twist: (1) Let passersby know it's your business; (2) dress creatively, even if that means a three-piece suit; and (3) give away free samples.

899. If one of your products is favorably mentioned in a publication or on a TV or radio show that is fairly well known, get stickers printed up with the endorsement printed on them and then include them on every item that you sell from that point on.

900. If your location and zoning laws permit, sell your product literally from your front yard. Dick Harrington builds sailboats by hand and sells them by placing one on his front lawn in Hancock, New Hampshire, with a For Sale sign. He usually has just one boat on the lawn at a time, and by the time the boat sells, the next boat that he's built is ready to replace it.

901. If you plan to do some door-to-door selling, avoid the "cold call" syndrome by sending a simple postcard

about your business to the targeted geographical area be-
forehand, or run a series of ads in the local paper. Carry
the postcard or ad with you when you solicit.

902. If you run a service-oriented business, discounting
your fees may not always be the best way to increase your
business. A premium fee, backed up by premium service,
may set your business apart from the competition. But
your customers have to feel they're getting value for their
dollars.

903. If you sell a product on consignment through a network of stores, increase the store's percentage by 5 to 10
percent if you can afford it. If they're making more money
by selling *your* product, you can be sure they'll promote
it.

904. If your city or town allows it, set up a booth at the
town square or on a busy street corner to promote your
business. One chiropractor in a major metropolitan area
gives away brochures about pain relief while promoting
his practice.

905. If you're selling a product or service that would
make a good Christmas or Hanukkah gift for companies
to give to their employees or customers, send a sample to
the head of the company in September, along with a catalog or brochure listing the benefits of such a gift.

906. If you're thinking of discounting your service or
product during the times that are slow, think again. One

beauty salon operator regularly cuts the prices of his most popular services when they are most in demand. This way, he brings in new customers who may become regular customers and therefore generate more revenue for him year round.

907. Virginia Wilson is a walking advertisement for her business. She sells fashion jewelry through home parties. But whenever she heads out to the local shopping mall, she wears lots of her beautiful jewelry. It doesn't take long until someone says, "I love your bracelet," and then she tells her that she wants her to have a piece just like it for free. At that point, she'll invite her to her next party and the gift—along with several sales—is made.

908. No matter if you're promoting your business through direct mail, a cold call, or by lecturing to thousands of people, you must always remember to *ask for the sale*. More than one entrepreneur has worked an audience into a lather and then left the stage without asking for their orders.

909. If your product is appropriate, set up a display with an informational brochure in the ladies' room at the mall, in restaurants, or in gas stations—do this with the cooperation of the management or they'll just get tossed. You'll have a captive audience in a heavy traffic area.

910. One restaurateur sends out congratulatory letters to employees at local businesses who have recently been promoted, offering them free champagne at his restaurants.

The company mails out about thirty letters a day, which costs a little over $1,600 per year; however, the return on investment is substantial: the promotion netted over $106,000 in revenue in 1995 alone, with a 29 percent response rate.

911. If there's an appropriate store in your area that will post your business card, try to do this in as many places as you can. For example, hardware stores have a bulletin board that is just covered with business cards of local tradespeople in the area. You never know who's going to walk into the store and need your services.

912. To get customers to switch from your competitor's business to yours requires a powerful incentive: One gasoline company not only accepts all its competitors' credit cards but gives new customers who sign up for their credit card the first three fill-ups on the house. They also offer regular discounts and other promotions to all their customers.

913. When it comes to thinking about retail outlets for your products, don't overlook unusual venues. Museums, for instance, will often carry items—from T-shirts to books to handmade crafts—that reflect the local history and culture. Truck stops would be good outlets for audiotapes or travel-related merchandise.

914. If you're looking for a sales rep in another part of the country, get a copy of a local paper or the Yellow Pages and look up the type of shop you'd like to have carry your products. Then call the shop, ask for the names of the reps they deal with, and then contact them.

915. Do like the Avon Lady does: give your brochure or catalog to a friend who works in a large company and have her pass the offer around the office. Offer a special deal and customizing for an even bigger response.

916. When you are on a sales call, the biggest mistake you can make is to hand out brochures or other promotional materials while you are talking. This gives the customer an excuse to become distracted and will lessen your chances of closing the sale. Some salespeople just hand out their business cards at the end of the sales call, which allows their performance to stand out in the minds of the customer and not the facts put forth in a brochure.

917. Whenever you go on a sales call, it helps if you're as sharp-eyed as possible. Compliment little touches that the customer has added to her place of business, and think of ways in which you can make these comments relevant to your product or service.

918. Send a singing telegram to a potential customer who's particularly tough to win over.

Packaging Your Product or Service

919. What can you do to make your business stand out? A business that is unique in itself usually has no problem attracting the attention of the media and, therefore, customers. One good example is a restaurant named Brannon's, in Cody, Wyoming. It has only five tables, it's only open on Friday and Saturday nights, from March through October, and it serves a prix fixe eight-course Italian feast with only one sitting a night. It's in the middle of nowhere, but the idea works—with a three-month waiting list for dinner—because the food is so good and the setting so romantic. Take this idea and vary it by promoting a special night or a special program at your business one night a week, or even one month out of the year.

920. To promote your business through your company vehicles, paint each one a distinctive color. One bakery in our area painted every one of its vans a deep lavender color that you couldn't find on any car. Therefore, they always stand out, which helps increase their visibility for current and future customers.

921. A slogan can be an effective marketing tool for a small business. One refrigerator service organization offers twenty-three-and-a-half-hour service and advertises this on their service vehicles. This unique twist on the usual round-the-clock service will catch most people's attention.

922. Build your business around a marketing theme that capitalizes on people's fears. For instance, one dentist advertises that his practice caters to chickens. In fact, the logo in all of his promotional materials is a chicken.

923. Can you package some of your products and/or services together to offer them to customers in a gift basket? An unusual mix—not the standard fruit and candy—may bring you a lot of attention from your current customer roster.

924. If you want to promote your business to a particular ethnic group or demographic profile, be sure that you are sincere about it and are extremely familiar with this market. Otherwise, you'll just turn people off.

925. A well-thought-out motto can position your business effectively because it's a succinct way to present your business to potential customers. Barbara Brabec, the author of *Homemade Money,* says that a motto is best used when it points to an unfilled niche in the market, or when it emphasizes something that is lacking in a competitor's product.

926. What makes your business unique, and what can you do to exploit it? Gary Calvert of Chestnut, Illinois, found out that his town is at the geographical center of the state. He used this as the basis for attracting tourists to the town. The general store in Chestnut now sells T-shirts, bumper stickers, pins, mugs, and caps that all extol the fact that the town is indeed at the geographical center of the state.

927. How can you position your marketing to take advantage of the new push in cellular communications? If your marketing targets busy people on the go, arrange with your local cellular phone company to include a brochure or other information about your company in every informational package it passes out to new customers.

928. If the businesses in your field aren't normally known for their "no questions asked" return policy, then be the first on your block to try it. Car America, a used-car dealership in Madison, Wisconsin, offers their customers the option of returning the car within three days with no questions asked, with the opportunity to exchange the vehicle for another within thirty days without charge.

929. If you are a service or information-oriented business, how many ways can you package your material in order to reach as wide a market as possible? Can you produce and sell a newsletter, then develop the information into a book or seminar, then go on-line or offer yourself as a business or personal consultant?

930. If your brilliant new marketing idea has been scooped by a competitor, don't necessarily abandon it completely. Consider how you can give it a fresh twist . . . a modestly high discount or better credit terms on a special promotion might be just enough. Other factors—such as your geographical locale, unique customer base, or the timing of the promotion—may encourage you to go forward with your plan.

931. If you sell a product with which 99 percent of consumers are familiar—like a hamburger or a taco—what can you do to make it stand out while retaining its original flavor? One company in the business of producing taco shells came up with the Tacone, a large-size taco in the shape of an ice cream cone, colored blue and green.

932. If your business is off the beaten path, your first marketing consideration should be what you can offer customers that more centrally located businesses cannot. Peace and quiet and lower prices—as a result of lower overhead—are just two of the more compelling pluses. Better service and longer hours are others.

933. If you're going after both wholesale and retail sales, you'll need to alter your approach to each. For instance, to entice innkeepers to sign up for a database of B&Bs for business travelers, a travel consulting firm offers them two special reports on how to market their businesses better. Consumers who buy the directory get free information on how to make their business travel experiences more enjoyable.

934. Offer a 100 percent money-back guarantee on your product or service, and then be sure to back it up with quality to match. There are companies like L. L. Bean, which has been known to give a customer her money back after having used a product for twenty years. Most guarantees will carry some limitations and still be effective marketing tools. Few people, if any, will take advantage of your offer over the course of a year.

935. Position yourself as the underdog and you may actually attract enough business to become number one. Avis tries harder and 7UP is the Uncola: these marketing strategies attract the many freethinkers who are suspicious of the giant player in the field.

936. Sometimes a very modest change in your product is a good excuse for a promotion. Changing the color or size of the packaging can be enough for a new campaign.

937. Would an appropriate "mascot" prove effective in bringing more business your way? It's worked with the Pillsbury Dough Boy and Planters Mr. Peanut. A "mascot" can become the focal point for your special events and advertising or inspire a product line all on its own.

938. What can you offer your customers that will make them both smile and remember you? A giveaway that you can refer to as a survival kit can contain a bottle of aspirin as well as a personalized pen or travel coffee mug with the name of your business imprinted on it that they can use at their office or at home. Personalize the kit with additional items that are pertinent to your customers' lives.

939. When designing the packaging that will best market your product, don't be afraid to stand out. People thought that Smart Food was crazy to use a black bag for its cheese popcorn, but it succeeded so well that the larger snack food companies have actually copied them.

940. Your marketing message should stress that you're selling a long-term relationship, not just a one-night stand. This strategy will help you gain the trust of new customers and generate repeat business.

941. You know how Whitman chocolates sells samplers that consist of four to six chocolates in a box? You can do the same thing by providing samplers of your products. Your customers will appreciate the chance to try out different items without the expense of buying each one separately.

Customer Service

942. Can you set up some kind of home-delivery service to make it easier for your customers to do business with you? Even if it's not a common service in your industry, give it a try.

943. Can you start a fan club for one of your products, services, or even one of your employees? This would be a fun, inexpensive way to reward loyal customers.

944. Consider establishing the equivalent of a "frequent flyer" program for your current customers. This should help to engender loyalty among many of your customers as well as attract new ones to the fold.

945. Here's a challenge for you in the way that you deal with both current and prospective customers. Answer "yes" to everything your customers ask for. Within reason, you should discover creative ways to satisfy every customer request.

946. How fast can you deliver your product or service to a buying customer? Offer alternatives, of course, from the traditional delivery schedules to same-day messengers. Of course, the customer will pay for it, but you may be surprised to see how many people do pay extra so they can get what they want fast.

947. If you have clients who come to you regularly and they are always asking to use your phone to check in with their office, you might want to set up a separate space just for these customers. It could be just an empty desk with a phone, a computer hookup, and fax. If these customers look at your business as an island in a storm, they will repay you with repeat and increased business.

948. If you run a business where customers must make appointments in person to deal with you, try this incentive: If a customer is kept waiting for more than fifteen minutes past his appointment, then there's no charge for that visit. Some urban banks offer cash to customers who have to wait in line for more than ten minutes.

949. Can your business go mobile? Customize a van—just as libraries have done for years—for your business, whether it's dog grooming, fitness training, or a beauty salon. One enterprising psychiatrist provides commuter limousine service and conducts her sessions with clients on the road.

950. If you're used to meeting with prospective and present customers one-on-one, find out the time of day and day of the week when they prefer to have meetings. While Friday afternoons are generally the poorest choice, some people like a midday break from their routine while others prefer the early-morning quiet.

951. In order to cultivate a loyal group of regular customers, create a club for them. Send out information about special sales and anecdotes about the store on a regular basis to all members. This will make them feel special, as if they belong to your family. It's important to offer significant discounts—at least 20 percent—to engender this loyalty. The information that the members of the club provide will also help you better define the image of your business.

952. No matter if you're talking to a member of the press or to a potential customer, you can promote your business effectively by cultivating the art of listening. A good listener asks questions. These questions lead to solutions to your customers' problems.

953. Offering your customers the opportunity either to pay on time installments or to lay away their purchase for the future are both valuable sales techniques, especially when many credit card users run their cards up to the limit.

954. Give your best customers books that are both timely and that contain information that's important to them.

955. Be flexible in the way you provide information to potential customers. If you normally like a face-to-face meeting, be sure to offer written materials for those people who prefer that. Many people are put off by what they think will be a high-pressure salesperson showing up at the door. Or they don't want to travel to your store just to find out the price of some advertised items.

956. Send out birthday cards to your customers; it's a nice touch that will gain more attention than the holiday cards that the majority of businesses send out.

957. Read the newspaper. Whenever you find an article or news item that is pertinent to one of your customers, send it along by fax or mail annotated by hand. This will not only show that you're concerned about them but also let them know that you're keeping up with what's going on in the world.

958. A Pennsylvania retailer decided to find out why a certain group of his customers hadn't shopped at his stores in over a year by calling them on the phone. Many of his former customers responded in detail, which helped him to focus on alleviating some of their grievances. When he then wrote back to these same former customers alerting them to the changes he had made—including the replacement of one of his store managers—the resulting increase in sales more than covered the cost of his research.

959. Whenever a customer wants a refund, give it to her promptly, with a twist: in addition to the refund or exchange, throw in a gift certificate toward a future purchase. This will help you retain them as regular customers.

960. If you run a mail-order business, put a sticker that says "Sent Within Two Hours of Your Order" on the box.

Market Research

961. A great way to find new customers is by checking the county government list of new business trade name registrations. As you know, when you start up a new business, there's lots of stuff and services you need to buy, so this could be quite a lucrative audience for you. Some small local newspapers publish these lists every month, but you can also go to your county government office to get the names.

962. Conducting research of focus groups that consist of both current and prospective customers is a good way to see if your marketing is on target. Offer a suitable incentive like a free meal and/or a gift certificate for your business to thank the participants for their time.

963. Contact either your state's economic development department or the tourism department to check for any studies that point to future trends in your state that you should be aware of. One group of small tourist-oriented businesses in Charlestown, New Hampshire, discovered a study that showed that the town's attractions could draw a sizable tourist base for the state. The group then formed the Charlestown Economic Development Association of Tourism and secured small grants to initiate some of the suggestions in the study. They created a number of events to draw tourists to the area, including a townwide yard sale, a Christmas Day open house, and a founders' day celebration.

964. Your market research should include advance calls to prospective customers before you make a major investment. For instance, if you plan to distribute via retail outlets, call the most likely prospects to seek their advice. Not only will you get valuable information but you will also establish a vital contact, one who'll be flattered that you sought him out for his expertise.

965. If you're in a service-oriented field, your client may be the best source of market information. Andrew Morrison, whose company, Nia Direct, helps corporations design direct marketing strategies, admits that "if I'm not familiar with the particular field, I'll tell the client that I don't want to waste our time or theirs on research. Since they likely already have a lot of in-house research about their industry I'll ask them to share that information with me." This efficient approach to marketing research helps to reduce the number of billable hours to a client, and saving money is frequently the best way you can market your business to a new customer.

966. Visit your local bookstore regularly to keep up-to-date on new publications—both books and magazines—that are pertinent to your business. You'll find valuable information not only in the business section but throughout the store. You'll see trends—angels, simplicity, spirituality, sports, media, etc.,—that may impact on the way you market and the way your customers respond.

967. Find yourself a role model or mentor: someone who is retired or who has changed businesses can give you objective advice and help to identify more opportunities and guide you to a better sense of what your clients really need.

968. Whenever you do market research to decide if you should go ahead with a new product or service, don't automatically count the respondents among your definite list of customers. One of the worst questions to put on a market research questionnaire is "Would you buy this product if it were available today?" Getting a 90 percent response rate in the affirmative has caused many entrepreneurs to rush out to bring the product to market without doing additional research. So beware of this early enthusiasm.

Making a Good Impression

969. If it's appropriate, offer a limited edition of a product that is signed by one or more of its creators. You can also continue to follow the lead of book authors by personalizing a message on each item.

970. If your customers have written you letters thanking you for how your business has helped make life easier for them, assemble those letters into clear plastic sleeves, insert them into a looseleaf notebook, and display it prominently in your waiting room.

971. Take testimonial letters from customers and arrange them in a collage to display on the wall by the cash register.

972. If you run a business-to-business company, ask another entrepreneur who has performed satisfactory work for your business to write you a testimonial letter about your company. Then you do the same for her.

973. If it doesn't already exist, produce a directory of resources for your field. It could prove to be valuable both to your customers and to your colleagues as well as to the media, who will come to regard you as an expert in your industry.

974. If none of your competitors are open on Sundays or evenings, be the exception and open your doors or schedule appointments for those times.

975. If one of your markets is college students, don't just post your flyers and brochures on campus bulletin boards. Place some brochures liberally around campus and tack them up on bulletin boards that are intended just for staff members.

976. If you have developed a niche market with your own product (and a solid mailing list), consider producing your own mail-order catalog which will include related products from others. Not only will you receive exposure for your product, but you'll also be able to finance future marketing plans to expand distribution for your product.

977. If you have a shop in a downtown area, but there's a big shopping mall a few miles away that's getting a lot of traffic, you might consider renting a kiosk or small booth to display a selection of your items or services. Be sure to include enticements that will tempt these customers to come to your main shop.

978. If you run a business located in a rural area, or you have a roadside mailbox, then paint or design your mailbox around the theme of your business. A local construction company designed its mailbox to resemble a crane, a body shop built theirs in the shape of a car, and a wedding planning group made theirs look like a wedding cake.

979. You only get one opportunity to make a good first impression. The sidewalk in front of your store should be swept clean every morning, the windows should be sparkling, and your front doorway unencumbered.

980. If you want to stress the vast selection of your stock, or the talent that lies behind the services that you offer, include this in your marketing information: "We sell products from all fifty states," or "Our employees have the combined experience of more than 250 years."

981. If you've won a prize or award in your field, make sure that all your customers and potential customers know about it. Send a press release to the appropriate media, notify your customers in your next mailing or newsletter, affix a stamp or label to your product packaging, and/or add the award citation to your advertising, letterhead, and business cards.

982. Even if you're selling your product via wholesalers or distributors, make it a point to establish contact directly with the major retailers. Your personal commitment to your product will often be the factor that convinces a retailer to carry and to promote your goods above a competitor's.

983. If you're planning to give away free samples of your product or service to build your business, make sure before you promote it that the free samples are of the highest quality. Otherwise, you'll be throwing your money away.

984. In Harvard Square, Cambridge, Massachusetts, there are singers, jugglers, mimes, and other performance artists who depend on the generosity of the passersby. Is it possible for you to market your business in a venue like this? Where there's any crowd gathered, you have an opportunity to market or sell your goods.

985. You can use the "backlash" to a popular trend or product to your advantage. For example, a group of disgruntled employees formed the Lead Pencil Club in response to the omnipresence of computers throughout their workplace.

986. A used-car dealership in western Vermont somehow got a gold Volkswagen Beetle onto a five-story-high post. On clear days, you can see it from the next town. It's even become a local tourist attraction.

987. Matchbooks are quickly becoming the dinosaur of promotional materials. However, whoever said there had to be matches inside? You can now find promotional items that *look* like matchbooks but really have notepaper, a shower cap, or even a condom inside.

988. Your "annual report" can be a valuable marketing tool. While many businesses are not required by shareholders or by law to issue such a document, your published commentary of the past year's highlights and upcoming events can engage your current and prospective customers. You can include promotional coupons in your report. You can use it as a media tool. It can be in the form of a newspaper insert. It will give your company credibility in the minds of customers, the competition, and the media.

989. One great way to promote your business is to place boxes and entry blanks that people can fill out to win a free item from your business. The possibilities are endless: I've seen a local restaurant place such a box in the waiting room of a car repair shop. Just be sure to pick up the entries from the box once a week.

990. Table tents—the little cards placed on each table that restaurants use to promote a particular beer brand and/or specials—can also be useful in promoting other businesses like yours. Work out a deal with the restaurant owner to place your own table tents on each table in the restaurant and then track the increase in business.

991. Vanity license plates for your car or truck are an inexpensive way to draw attention to your business.

992. When other entrepreneurs and businesses are reducing the size and/or quality of their product or service, you should head in the opposite direction and increase your quantity and quality. The resulting boost in business should more than cover your increased expenses.

993. For your good customers, round *down* the amount of their purchases. For instance, if their total comes to $8.14, charge them only $8. It costs you pennies but will thrill your customers.

994. Whether you are exhibiting at a trade show or looking for a way to spice up business at your storefront, don't overlook the use of a neon sign to attract customers. Neon is an immediate attention-getter and is much more visible than traditional signs.

995. Always be on the lookout for what seems to be the next big trend. Phone cards burst out of nowhere in 1995, and almost overnight, a slew of multilevel marketing companies appear to have sprung up overnight to use them as a marketing tool. Keep up on the news to learn about what could be the next big thing.

Your Employees

996. If you rely on sales reps, whether they're independent or work directly for you, you should regularly think up personalized ways to reward them. For instance, some sales reps love to travel and would welcome a trip to some exotic place. Others might prefer gifts for the home. Most prefer cash.

997. Remember that your sales reps are an extension of your company. In order to keep them motivated, you must keep them notified of any new products or news about your company. Fax them copies of your press clips, newsletters, and new product descriptions so they in turn can share them with their customers. Excitement is contagious, and they can naturally convey this to their accounts.

998. Make employees feel as though they are responsible for the success of your business. To start with, assign them responsibility in one area, increasing it as they show progress.

999. One of the best ways to motivate your employees is to send them to at least one industry trade show and conference each year. This will show them that you value their skills, and they will bring back new ideas on how to increase your business. It's also a good idea to enroll them in the appropriate associations and subscribe to the magazines and other publications that will help them do their job better.

1,000. To stimulate sales, award bonuses to your employees based on performance. Whether it's a $100 bonus to salespeople if they meet a quota during a particular day, or a prize of up to $500 for an employee who produces the largest percentage of that day's revenues, contests—if used on an occasional basis—can go a long way toward keeping your staff people excited and your revenues up.

1,001. Give this book to all your employees. Ask them to look through it for ideas that they like most . . . and let them give those ideas a try!